Mary
Pathway to Fruitfulness

Mary
Pathway to Fruitfulness

LIVING FLAME PRESS
LOCUST VALLEY, N Y 11560

Cover: Lawrence Mellyn

Illustration: Susan Mellyn

Nihil Obstat: Rev. Msgr. John F. Cox, Ph.D. Censor Librorum, July 26, 1978

Imprimatur: Louis E. Gelineau, D.D., S.T.L., J.C.L., Bishop of Providence, July 28, 1978

ISBN: 0-914544-28-4

Printed in the United States of America

Dedication

To the Holy Spirit who,
when he finds a Mary heart,
hastens there
to bring forth the greatest fruit —
Jesus Christ

Contents

Foreword

Nobody wants to be a failure. Everyone wants to bear fruit. In John 15:18 Jesus tells us that it is to his Father's glory that "we bear much fruit and become his disciples."

In our lived experience at St. Patrick's parish in Providence, Rhode Island, the Holy Spirit showed us a remarkable pathway to this fruitfulness in the person of Mary, his Spouse. As the dedication of this work notes, "when he finds a Mary heart he hastens there to bring forth his greatest fruit — Jesus Christ."

Let me provide the background to this lived experience I speak of. In 1971 God began a remarkable renewal of parish life at St. Patrick's (cf. *In God's Providence, The Birth of a Catholic Charismatic Parish,* Living Flame Press, 1974) through the raising up of a Christian community deeply dedicated to prayer and afire with the Holy Spirit. I can't speak for other communities, but I can say that in this one the Holy Spirit unmistakably pointed us along the pathway of devotion to Mary as the way he wanted us to go in order to bear rich fruit. In her person, newly understood and appreciated, lay secret upon secret of fruitfulness. A veritable fountain of teaching soon emerged that gave abundant life. The three articles included here are but a sampling of this vitality.

Interestingly enough, we learned that St. Patrick's had originally been dedicated to Mary Conceived Without Sin as principal patroness of the parish — and this before 1854 when the dogma of the Immaculate Conception was declared in Rome. We marveled at the one Spirit acting then and now — ever new, ever old.

This ever-fresh Spirit taught us new approaches to an old devotion and then revitalized our lives. In the process he removed a lot of the alienations people felt toward Mary — alienations stemming from past immature teaching, a failure to grow beyond one's childhood experience of Mary, and what was often a shift of emphasis in Marian devotion following the Second Vatican Council. These alienations removed, we were freed to unlock the rich treasures Christians have always found in this beautiful garden called Mary.

Each of the three authors in this work offers an interesting glimpse into the rich personality of Mary. Helen Hawkinson, housewife and mother of two, presently the directress of a home for battered women and a good example of how fruitful a pathway Mary can be, speaks very practically of all the relationships Mary embraced: child, wife, mother, cousin. It is a novel approach and full of amazing insights for day-to-day Christian living at home and in the marketplace.

Sharyn Malloy, now on the staff of the Spiritual Life Center in Pawtucket, Rhode Island, is single and has an M.A. in Biblical Studies. She examines in a more scholarly fashion Mary's role as a suffering servant of the Lord, a solid and biblical model for us all to follow.

Finally, my own article attempts to bring us to the heart of fruitful living: the great commandment of love and the cross. It attempts to draw upon several unusual and ecumenical sources to show us how to come into new power in Gospel living.

All three articles attempt to build bridges: a bridge between Mary and Catholics, particularly those disaffected in their former devotion to Mary; and a bridge between Mary and other Christians, a bridge whose building is long overdue. This latter bridge promises to be exciting. Biblically, experientially, and ecumenically based, it has tremendous promise. The mother will gather her children from all parts!

The work reminds me of the phrase of Jesus in Matthew 13:52: "Every scribe who is learned in the Kingdom of God is like the head of a household who can bring out from his storeroom both the new and the old."

We would like to acknowledge all those who so richly have fed us the bread of the Word. A particular note of thanks to Sister Kieran Flynn, R.S.M. Finally we'd like to especially thank all who contributed to putting together this little book: Larry Mellyn for his cover design, Imelda St. George and Rose MacLure, who did much of the typing. May God give them all a Mary heart.

Fr. John Randall

Mary, the Model Relative
by Helen Prendergast Hawkinson

The cradle Catholic, outgrowing a small child-mother relationship with Mary, the mother of Jesus, often speaks of "lost devotion" sadly but irrevocably. That is most unfortunate because the child can love the Blessed Mother, but it requires maturity to begin to understand Mary's greatness.

In Scripture we find a portrait of Mary, drawn with few strokes, but revealing a woman of deep faith maturing from an obedient adolescent to a widow of incredible strength.

Mary is uniquely, extraordinarily favored by God. As the Spouse of the Holy Spirit and mother of the Messiah, she is the Daughter of Zion who can rejoice that the Lord is with her. Her position in the history of the human race is singular.

But Mary's life, in the day-to-day living of it, was quite ordinary, similar to the life experience of women in her era and throughout time. She married at an early age and had a child. Her husband was a working man, a carpenter.

According to the standards of their society, they were not a wealthy or powerful family. Later Jesus was judged by their lack of social importance when, as a man returning to his hometown to preach and heal, he was rejected for his "humble beginnings." The townspeople asked, "Who is he?" When they realized he was the son of Joseph, the carpenter, they refused to listen to Jesus or to believe in him because he was no one of importance, according to their standards. Jesus left after curing a few who were ill. He was a prophet dishonored in his own country.

Mary's daily work was that of poor women in all times. It is this commonality that helps us see Mary as a model as wife, mother, cousin, daughter, or as the Model Relative in general. In our age of fragmented families, relationships are vulnerable to instantaneous severing. More than ever before mankind needs to find models of ongoing, successful relating. There is Mary. She moved among God's people recognizing and responding to the needs of others, all the others sent into her life by God's plan.

We find Mary in the ordinary, but the quality of peace present in her life was extraordinary. As wife, mother, daughter, friend, she was without sin. We work out our salvation in some or all of these relationships. Mary did it all, and she did it perfectly. Throughout her life, in joy and in sorrow, she kept her heart open to the Word of God. She remained obedient to his plan, full of grace.

Each of us comes into the world carrying a message from God. The unique combination of gifts and talents endowing the newborn carries the invitation and the capability of answering yes to the life plan. Those who listen, hear. Those who hear, answer. Sometimes deciding that yes is the only answer does violence to the self, even though saying yes will bring peace. If saying no causes sadness or embarrassment, one tries to avoid that by saying nothing or by deciding to weigh it all carefully and answer nothing. The ultimate no is refusing to hear at all, to deafen one's ears.

Mary received a "call" or an invitation from God. She heard and responded.

References to Mary in the New Testament are few and brief. The evangelists' purpose was entirely Christ-centered, to tell about Jesus — what he said, what he did, who he was. Both Luke and Matthew begin their Gospels with an account of the birth of Jesus, positioning the man Jesus in place and time. Luke's Infancy Narrative serves as a bridge between the Old Testament and the New Testament. Alluding to Scripture and biblical in style, Luke 1-2 communicates the coming of the Messiah, the Promised One. In the process Luke leaves us a portrait of Mary, the mother of Jesus, depicting her humanity with its fears, feelings, and limitations.

Luke begins his Gospel with an account of the

conception of John the Baptist, whose mother, Elizabeth, is a relative of Mary's. When Elizabeth was in the sixth month of her pregnancy, "the angel Gabriel was sent from God to a town of Galilee named Nazareth to a virgin betrothed to a man named Joseph, of the house of David. The virgin's name was Mary" (*Luke 1:26-27*).

Mary was a young girl, perhaps fourteen or fifteen years old. She knew God as her Creator and her Lord. She was open-hearted to the Spirit of God and a good listener to the voice of her Lord.

In Luke 1:28 the angel Gabriel says, "Rejoice, O highly favored daughter! The Lord is with you. Blessed are you among women."

Luke does not depict Mary as a plaster of paris saint, serenely untouched by the arrival of an angel bearing a cryptic message. On the contrary, Luke describes her as "deeply troubled by his [Gabriel's] words" and says that she "wondered what his greeting meant."

Gabriel tells her not to be afraid. Obviously, she was afraid and needed reassurance, and it was given.

"Do not fear, Mary. You have found favor with God. You shall conceive and bear a son and give him the name Jesus. Great will be his dignity and he will be called the Son of the Most High. The Lord God will give him the throne of David his father. He will rule over the house of Jacob forever and his reign will be without end."

When Mary spoke, she asked a question. We

17

see her confused, wanting to understand what was being said to her but not understanding at all. The question she asks is not theological or intellectual. It is simple and practical. "How can this be since I do not know man?"

Gabriel, in response to her question, announced the mystery of the Virgin Birth. Mary was the first human to hear of God's exact plan of the entry of the Messiah into the world. This was the time. She was the vessel. Just as the ark of the covenant bore the Spirit of God as the Israelis moved across the desert, so she would bear God made flesh. She would be the living ark of the covenant. Gabriel answered, "The Holy Spirit will come upon you and the power of the Most High will overshadow you; hence, the holy offspring to be born will be called Son of God (*Luke 1:35*).

Gabriel could have left at that point. The message had been conveyed; the mystery was declared. All that was needed was Mary's consent, because God chooses to respect his children's free will. The mother of the Messiah would not be so unwillingly or unwittingly.

But God is a loving Father. As an encouragement to his young daughter, who was still troubled, God's messenger added, "Know that Elizabeth your kinswoman has conceived a son in her old age; she who was thought to be sterile is now in her sixth month, for nothing is impossible with God" (*Luke 1:36-37*).

The news about Elizabeth was as welcome as

it was startling. Sterility was considered a great shame among the Jews. Elizabeth had prayed for years that the Lord would give her a child. Her relatives, no doubt, had prayed for her. And now Mary heard that all their prayers had been answered. Elizabeth, after all the years of praying, of hoping, of longing, was going to have a son in her old age. Mary knew of other Jewish women who had sons in their old age. There was Sarah, who bore Isaac, the son promised to Abraham, the father of the Jewish people. There was Hannah, who bore Samuel, the great prophet who anointed David, the king of the Jewish people. And now there was Elizabeth, her kinswoman.

Gabriel's final words reached Mary's heart: "For nothing is impossible with God." She believed that. The process of our redemption had reached a crucially important stage. Mary did not know the theology of salvific history. But Mary did know the role of the daughter of the Most High. She understood the relationship. And Mary said, "I am the servant of the Lord. Let it be done to me as you say." She made an act of complete, total acceptance. She said, "I am a creature of God. I am his servant, his slave, his child. God is my Creator, my Lord, my Father." Whatever she is, God has given her, and she gives it all back to him. "I am the handmaid of the Lord; whatever God wants, let that be done." She may not understand it all. She might not have chosen this plan for her life if she were

Creator, but she is not Creator. God is God. She is his child and she is at peace with God's revealed plan. There is no death-dealing tension in Mary between what she wants and what God wants. She has agreed. Let it be done. And our Redeemer was conceived in her womb and became flesh.

The obedient daughter affirms the plan of her Father. She did not know all the details of God's plan. The full meaning would unfold before her all the days of her life, but Mary agreed to trust God's love, to trust God's faithfulness. She agreed that whatever God wants, she wants. The daughter of the Most High agrees to become mother of the Messiah. The relationship Mary has with God influences and colors all her other relationships. It is an integral part of each of them.

As we search Scripture for Marian references, we realize that what the Holy Spirit inspired and men wrote includes Mary at moments in her life that are highly pertinent to our lives. She is hearing, answering, learning, living out a situation with universal implications. Mary's inclusion in the "living Word" is always a witness to us. She is creature, child of God, hearing the Creator's call, and answering.

Cousin of Elizabeth

"Thereupon Mary set out, proceeding to hasten into the hill country to a town of Judah, where she entered Zechariah's house and greeted Elizabeth" (*Luke 1:39*).

During the fifty- or sixty-mile journey to Elizabeth's house, Mary had time to think, to doubt, to reconsider, to examine. Imagine the range of thoughts possible to such a young girl. Did she really experience divine revelation, or did she imagine it all? Was it pride that led her to religious fantasy, casting herself in the role of the mother of the Savior of her people? But no, she knew. In the peace at the center of her being, she knew.

God had a great gift waiting for Mary. When Elizabeth heard Mary's voice, the baby leaped in her womb and the Holy Spirit filled Elizabeth. She cried out in a loud voice, "Blest are you among women and blest is the fruit of your womb. But who am I that the mother of my Lord should come to me? The moment your greeting sounded in my ears, the baby leaped in my womb for joy. Blest is she who trusted that the Lord's words to her would be fulfilled."

Elizabeth knew! She knew Mary was pregnant, and she knew who her child was! The Holy Spirit moved Elizabeth to cry out, "The mother of my Lord." Elizabeth knew nothing of the historical Jesus. We have nearly two thousand years of tradition and Gospel behind our thinking. But when Elizabeth said, "The mother of my Lord," she didn't refer to the God-man Jesus; she spoke of the Most High God. The mystery must have been incomprehensible to her as she said the words. But she knew, without knowing how she knew, and she spoke in confirmation of the angel's message.

Luke records Mary's response as a prayer of thanksgiving, which is composed of Old Testament phrases. As we read Luke 1:46, we find Mary. The verses did not originate with Mary, but they are identified with her so strongly that their earlier usage is dimmed by comparison.

My being proclaims the greatness of the Lord, my spirit finds joy in God my saviour,

For he has looked upon his servant in her lowliness; all ages to come shall call me blessed.

God who is mighty has done great things for me, holy is his name;

His mercy is from age to age on those who fear him. He has shown might with his arm; he has confused the proud in their inmost thoughts.

He has deposed the mighty from their thrones and raised the lowly to high places.

The hungry he has given every good thing, while the rich he has sent empty away.

He has upheld Israel his servant, ever mindful of his mercy;

Even as he promised our fathers, promised Abraham and his descendants forever.

Mary praised God. She rejoiced in God, her Lord, her Savior. Then she stated the reality of her situation. God had chosen her from among all the women born throughout the ages. She didn't say it wasn't possible and that she wasn't worthy. She knew that nothing is impossible with God. Mary accepted reality, and the reality was that God had chosen her to be the mother of the Savior. Without pride, without self-glorification, Mary stated the truth. God had given her a great gift. She spoke about it in a manner characteristic of Mary by giving the glory to God. Mary accepted Elizabeth's praise, but she took it right to the source, to God. Mary is God-centered. And Elizabeth praised Mary because she trusted that the Lord's promise to her would be fulfilled. And so it was.

How many times has God called us? Sometimes we answer, "Let it be done" or "Here I am, Lord; send me." Other times we may throw the roadblock of false humility clear across the road we are walking with the Lord. "I can't. I'm not good enough, or old enough, or wise or holy or strong enough. God couldn't use me. He will have to find someone else better suited." And after judging God and finding him to have slightly less common sense than we, or else refusing to accept that the invitation is from God, we refuse to answer. It is difficult for most of us to realize that God does want to use us, to work through us, to be one with us.

One icy day last winter, I drove down Smith

Street to Our Daily Bread Food Coop. Usually I am an optimistic driver, go directly to my destination, and then search for a place to park. This particular day I began circling about a block from the coop and doubled back aimlessly, wondering as I did why I was going out of my way. Then I spotted a woman I knew slightly standing in the rain waiting for a bus. I pulled in without even considering what I was doing, opened the car door, and asked her if I could drive her someplace. There were tears in her eyes as she got into the car. "Do you know what I was doing there at the bus stop? I was praying," she said. "Last night I stayed up late with a friend whose husband just died. This morning I had a very important appointment, but I overslept. When I called they said I had to come by noon. It is almost that now, and I just said to God, 'Please send someone to help me. Send someone to drive me, because the bus is late, and I need to be downtown in a few minutes.' As soon as I finished saying that, you pulled over and offered me a ride." She and I both knew that I was God's answer to her prayer. The station wagon, which has been cursed more than blessed, and I, unworthy in my own eyes, were sent to minister to a beautiful child of God. An immediate love formed between us, not because of the ride needed and given, but because God brought us together at that moment in time. She prayed. God answered. I was the answer. God revealed his love for each of us through the other at that moment.

Later, thinking about the incident, I felt very humble. God loves this woman very much. She is precious in his sight. Prayer is an important part of her life, and out of her prayer come many good works, small kindnesses and great acts of charity. What does worldly wisdom tell us? If you want something done right, do it yourself. If you want a message delivered right, go yourself. Now God did want something done right, but he sent me. The way God works is to send me, and others like me, when he calls us to his plan. A simple mission such as giving someone a ride downtown wouldn't upset most of us or cause false humility to obstruct with "I am not worthy." But this simple mission showed me that God chooses to work through me in small things and in great things according to his plan, his design. Nothing is impossible with God. If Mary could accept the role of mother of Jesus with humility, we can learn from her to accept any role, any mission, any gift with humility.

At the Southern New England Regional Service Conference in Rhode Island in May 1977, Father George Kosicki, homilist at the Mass on Sunday told us he heard himself calling Jesus "the humble one." He had been praying with his brother priests at the Bethany House of Intercessory Prayer for Priests, in Warwick, Rhode Island. Suddenly he heard himself praising Jesus saying, "You are the humble one." He had not referred to Jesus in that way before and spoke about it later to another priest on the team at Bethany House. His teammate replied, "What does that mean? That must mean Jesus is humble because he uses you, George." The hundreds of us in the audience laughed at that. It was a good, happy, warm joke. Because God does use George Kosicki. Those of us who have heard him speak do not doubt that God anoints him. And Jesus is the humble one. He will use each of us, if we are humble enough to accept. If we are humble enough, God will make us great. Mary knew that, and she praised God.

We read in Luke that Mary stayed with Elizabeth for three months. What a blessing to Elizabeth during the third tripartem of her pregnancy to have Mary, and the Lord within her, present in the house.

Let's consider the practical aspects of Mary's visit to Elizabeth. Elizabeth was an older woman, pregnant for the first time. While she naturally rejoiced that the "curse of sterility" was lifted from her, she just as naturally wondered why it could not have all come to pass twenty years earlier. She had lived her life, up to that point, quite unaware of God's plan that her child's birth would closely precede the birth of her young cousin's child. Her cousin Mary was not even born when Elizabeth, a young bride, longed for a child. The sorrow of her young womanhood was necessary if she were to enter into God's glorious plan for her and her husband, Zechariah, a plan that necessitated the birth of their first child in their old age, a plan that occasioned the visit of her young cousin whose vision she would confirm. And yet the sorrow had been real. Elizabeth had been sterile until she was an old woman.

Now Elizabeth was pregnant. Her household chores were hard to keep up. And there was little help. Her mother, if she were still living, would have been quite ancient. Her husband, Zechariah, had returned from the temple one day unable to speak, and he had not regained the power of speech the nine months following. He had his own problems to cope with. Elizabeth was tired. Her water jug grew heavier. Washing clothes on the rocks was increasingly difficult.

God, the loving Father of this precious daughter Elizabeth, did not ignore her burden. He did not treat her as pure spirit. He made her and he knew her, body, soul and spirit. And God sent her a young, strong, peaceful girl who could do the wash and fill the water jugs, and bake the bread and rub Elizabeth's back. He sent her a prayerful, loving girl who could transmit God's love to Zechariah and Elizabeth, who could pray for them and with them, who could receive guests peacefully, calmly and with full confidence that God held them in the palm of his hand.

How many neighbors must have congratulated Elizabeth on the arrival of her young cousin! She could have had no better maidservant if she lived in the palace. They did not know Mary was the mother of the Lord. But Elizabeth knew. Mary had come to care for Elizabeth, and she cared as only one close to the Lord can care, with anointed love.

Wife of Joseph

Luke, after recording that Mary stayed with Elizabeth for three months and then returned home, next mentions Joseph and Mary travelling to Bethlehem where Jesus is born. No account is given of the remaining six months of Mary's pregnancy in Luke's gospel. More references to Mary and Joseph's relationship can be found in Matthew. Before looking at Matthew's Infancy Narrative, it would be good to review Mary's situation when she returned from her cousin Elizabeth's home.

Three months earlier, Mary had agreed to become the mother of the Lord. The Holy Spirit "overshadowed" her, the child was conceived in her womb, Mary was pregnant.

At that time Mary and Joseph had already signed a marriage contract and were given to each other by their parents, according to the custom prevailing. They were not engaged, or promised to each other for a future marriage. They were contracted, given to each other. It was customary to wait a year between the first ceremony, the signing of the contract, and the second ceremony, the consecration of the marriage, if the girl was a young virgin. Joseph had planned accordingly to wait a year before taking Mary into his home.

Mary naturally looked forward to her life with Joseph, the joys of married life, and hoped for the blessing of many children. In primitive or agrarian societies children can, by their labor, increase the prosperity of the family; by their strength or cleverness, increase the family's power; and by their family loyalty, provide for their aged parents when they are no longer able to work hard. Therefore, children were a great blessing in Mary and Joseph's society.

Yet at the moment she said, "Let it be done unto me as you say," Mary agreed to become the mother of a child which was not fathered by Joseph. And according to Catholic Scripture scholars, she had agreed to remain a virgin all her life.

Now how was she to explain all of this to Joseph? She was pregnant with a child conceived by God, not by her husband or any other man. She was a virgin and would remain so all of her life. She was Joseph's wife and would be consecrated in marriage as planned, but both of them would have to accept a life of celibacy for eschatological reasons.

All of this was agreed upon without Joseph's knowledge or consent. God had called and Mary said, "Yes." In a society where women had very few rights, where they were used as chattel by their fathers and their husbands, no young girl could have made such an agreement unless she was a believer. Mary believed. She believed in God's love; she trusted in his mercy; she hoped in his providence. Mary was, therefore, able to answer yes to God's invitation to her. But there was still the ordeal of telling Joseph.

We think of this situation from our vantage point two thousand years later. Our image of Joseph, formed by Christmas plays and statues on the side altars of our childhood churches, reveals a finished product, a complete saint with nothing left to work out. But Mary knew Joseph. He was flesh and blood and personality.

Mary could not be certain that Jopseh would understand and accept her pregnancy. Joseph was a good man, but how many good men have been hard pressed to understand the feelings their wives say they are experiencing, or comprehend the reality their wives claim exists? How many good men hearing Mary's story would want to believe her, but find it impossible? Perhaps one might conclude that she thought she was telling the truth because the reality of what she had done was too horrible to face and she had blotted it out of her mind. How many good men would go off sorrowfully and quietly make arrangements to put the girl away or send her away to have her baby, perhaps even providing support for her but not wanting to see her again? Sex before marriage was not a debatable topic among the Jews. It was a crime, punishable by stoning. Joseph was a good man, and he decided to send Mary away quietly, not charging her with adultery, not having her face death by stoning, but surely not taking her into his home as his wife.

Mary could not rely completely on Joseph's goodness or his wisdom or his love or his compassion. It was there, but it was finite. It was limited and clouded. Mary could not place her trust in Joseph assuming he was perfect. He wasn't. But he was her husband. God had given him to her as husband, as foster father of her God-child. And Mary could trust in God. "Be it done unto me according to your will. . . ." Her life was in God's hands. Mary trusted in God's ability to handle the problems surrounding her pregnancy. Whatever God wanted, Mary wanted. She could thank God for the circumstances in her life, and he could intervene freely in her life. Mary did not block God by trying to handle the impossible herself. She let God be God, while she thanked him for his loving care. "He has looked upon his servant in her lowliness." And God intervened.

In Matthew 1:20 we read: ". . . suddenly an angel of the Lord appeared in a dream and said to him: 'Joseph, son of David, have no fear about taking Mary as your wife. It is by the Holy Spirit that she has conceived this child. She is to have a son and you are to name him Jesus because he will save his people from their sins.' "

Matthew refers to Joseph as "an upright man," that is, one who is law abiding, living according to the Law of the Jewish people, and in that sense a just man. The justice of Mosaic Law would have been violated if Joseph married Mary knowing full well he was not the father of her child and that she was guilty of adultery. If he quietly divorced her, she would fall victim to gossip, to charges, and perhaps even punishment as an adulteress. God's messenger assured Joseph that Mary was innocent of adultery and that marrying her into his home would not be contrary to the law. And we read in Matthew 1:24, "When Joseph awoke he did as the angel of the Lord had directed him and received her into his home as his wife. He had no relations with her at any time before she bore a son, whom he named Jesus."

Some scholars attribute Joseph's fear not to a concern that Mary was guilty of adultery, but rather to an awareness of the truth and a belief that he was unworthy to invite her and the divine infant in her womb into his home as wife and child. The angel's message tells Joseph that he is chosen to do that when it is announced, "You are to name him Jesus." The father normally named the child. Joseph is invited to incorporate Jesus into his family, his line, the house of David, by the act of naming him. This would be equivalent to adoption.

The important lesson here is that Joseph heard and answered God, accepting the role Almighty God had chosen him to fill. Mary and Joseph individually and jointly trusted God.

It would be wrong for us to assume, however, that at the moment of the Incarnation Joseph was drawn into the mystery. If we do, we minimize Mary's walk in faith by denying her problem. We would be suggesting that she didn't need to trust in God for solutions because they came to her without delay, without her enduring all things in blind faith in God's goodness. Mary's faith was strengthened in testing. She knew that in her marriage she could trust God and walk patiently before her Father and he would work out the changes of heart needed, while he gave the grace of love and understanding.

Any two people committed to each other in marriage approach crossroads on life's path. At times they will happily read the same "signs" at the same time. At other times, one will see a sign in the distance and, tugging the other by the sleeve, cry out, "Don't you see? Can't you understand? It is so clear to me, so obvious. Why won't you understand?"

The other partner may echo each question inwardly, wishing desperately to see the sign that is so obvious, so clear to the other but clouded or invisible, or worse still, reversed in his mind's eye.

And still they are committed to each other. These two, who are made one, cannot sever themselves and part at each crossroads where one perceives differently than the other. And they can stay together praying: "Oh Lord, if it is your truth I am holding in my heart, let him hear it too. Please help him to know what you have told me. It hurts to see that which others do not see. Send your Spirit of truth on us that we may see together." Or at other times, "Lord, help her to know and understand what you are telling me. I don't want her to resign herself, to submit. I want her to accept because she knows too. I want her to see what I see. Help her to see together with me."

And the Lord answers such painful cries for unity and helps them to focus together, bringing the next stage of the journey into the light. Lives of quiet desperation corroded with bitterness, anger, and resentment can be cleansed and restored through prayer.

How many months did it take before Joseph realized that Mary's child was conceived by the Holy Spirit? We don't know when, other than that it was in God's time. And we know too that Mary had known the truth every hour, every day of the intervening time. She was not tense or ridden with anxiety. Luke 1:47: "My spirit finds joy in God my savior."

Mary trusted in God. She was filled with joy that Joseph knew, when he did know, and that he agreed and was at peace. Her joy was not diluted with regrets that it did not happen earlier or differently. God's plan was Mary's plan. If this was his time, then let it be.

The joy and peace in Mary and Joseph's marriage didn't flow from power, wealth, or worldly goods. They were not rich in security or stability in an economic sense. Both Luke and Matthew in writing of the birth of Jesus record political unrest and hardship.

Luke positions the birth of Jesus in the world at large, not just in the Jewish nation. Accordingly he begins with Augustus, emperor of Rome, "ordering a census of the whole world." Joseph and Mary had to register in Bethlehem, the city of Joseph's family, the house of David. In Luke we see Mary and Joseph travelling ninety miles to Bethelehem from Nazareth. Caesar had ordered a census and his power extended from Rome, down the power structure of the empire, into its occupied territories, and into the lives of Mary and Joseph, who complied with the edict. The poor do not have friends who can intervene for them, making their compliance unnecessary. But even as they made a difficult journey, Mary and Joseph experienced peace. Where could they find peace in that situation? Only in knowing that Caesar would have no authority over them if God had not given it to him. Only in trusting that this was God's plan for them, and if it were not he would intervene. Only in keeping their hearts centered on God could they find peace and joy on the hard journey.

Bethlehem was crowded when they arrived. It isn't difficult to imagine those who were able positioning themselves in the center of things, observing and analyzing the wealth of the other illustrious sons of the house of David. Mary and Joseph could not expect great comfort, but certainly they hoped to find shelter; certainly they prayed for a place to stay, where Mary could give birth to the savior of the world.

In Luke we read, "While they were there the days of her confinement were completed. She gave birth to her first-born son and wrapped him in swaddling clothes and laid him in a manger, because there was no room for them in the place where travelers lodged" (*Luke 2:6-7*).

God, who is all loving, provided for his Son's birth. He provided a cave where animals were kept, and a manger for a crib.

Mary could not rely on Joseph's ability to provide. Together, Joseph and Mary relied on God's desire and ability to provide that which was the greatest good. This time it was a stable. Stables were for animals, for beggars and servants, and for God.

Stables were also comfortable places for shepherds. God wanted some shepherds to be among the first to know and to see the Word made flesh. Once again the poor, ragged, lowly outcasts and drifters were chosen by God. The good news would be preached to the poor.

Matthew signifies the universal mission of Christ by the arrival of Gentiles, astrologers who stopped at the palace of Herod in Jerusalem asking, "Where is the newborn king of the Jews? We observed his star at its rising and have come to pay him homage."

Matthew tells us that "At this news King Herod became greatly disturbed, and with him all of Jerusalem." A new king born with a star announcing his arrival could be a serious problem. It might signify the end of the ruling house or a change in the social order, jeopardizing Herod's position, power, wealth, and comfort. Plans needed to be made and steps taken to protect the status quo. Those who have much to lose frequently have a peculiar affection for the system that provides their privileges. Herod was especially jealous of his power and immediately called in the scribes and the chief priests to cull any information which would narrow the search, ostensibly for the astrologers (the Magi), but certainly for himself as well. The information was quickly forthcoming. The Messiah was to be born in Bethlehem of Judah. "Here is what the prophet has written: 'And you, Bethlehem, land of Judah, are by no means least among the princes of Judah, since from you shall come a ruler who is to shepherd my people Israel.' "

After dispatching the astrologers with expressions of his desire to go and pay homage to the newborn king and an invitation to return to his palace with exact details of the child's birth, Herod most likely initiated his own quiet investigation. But the local cognoscenti hadn't a scrap of information. There was no one among their illustrious acquaintances who fit the description, and there was no need to look beyond themselves. They were, after all, the outstanding families and from their number a King Messiah would come, if he came at all.

The astrologers made their pilgrimage to the child and his parents, perhaps in the cave Luke refers to as the birthplace, but certainly ignored, unnoticed by most of the visitors to Bethlehem.

Later the astrologers returned to their homes without reporting back to Herod. Matthew writes (2:13), "After they had left, the angel of the Lord suddenly appeared in a dream to Joseph with the command: 'Get up, take the child and his mother, and flee to Egypt. Stay there until I tell you otherwise. Herod is searching for the child to destroy him.' Joseph got up and took the child and his mother and left that night for Egypt." Herod, in a rage, dispatched his people to find the child. Failing in that, he ordered the slaughter of all male children in Bethlehem under the age of two.

In Luke we see Mary and Joseph arrive in Bethlehem, needing shelter. They accepted the stable God provided as the greatest good. It was not a palace but if it was a gift from God, then it was the right gift. Another gift from God was the wisdom that saved their lives when Joseph was warned to take the child and Mary and get out of Herod's reach.

Mary's life was a daily dependence on God and on Joseph who listened to the Lord. They travelled thirty miles from Bethlehem across Sinai to El Qantara, which means the bridge.

This ancient crossing about five miles south of the Mediterranean and north of the Gulf of Suez was the Holy Family's route into exile in Egypt. For the sake of the Savior, who would redeem the world, Mary and Joseph became political exiles.

During the brief stay in Egypt (perhaps two or three years), Mary heard the Lord speak to her through Joseph. Twice more Matthew sets Joseph in a dream in which he receives directions, once to return to Israel and later to go to Galilee where he settled his family in Nazareth. Little is known about their family life in Nazareth, but it is certain they were without wealth and without the power, ease, and cultural advantage wealth can procure.

Once more we see Mary and Joseph together in Luke's Gospel. When Jesus was about twelve years old, his parents lost him during a trip to Jerusalem. After searching three days, first in the caravan leaving the city and later in Jerusalem itself, they found Jesus in the temple sitting among the teachers asking amazingly mature and intelligent questions.

Mary's sorrow at being separated from Jesus finds expression in the question, "Son, why have you done this to us? You see that your father and I have been searching for you in sorrow." (We will look at this verse again in reference to Mary's relationship with Jesus.) And again in Luke 2:51: "He went down with them then, and came to Nazareth, and was obedient to them."

Both of these verses suggest a unity between Mary and Joseph that was deep and strong. Almost thirteen years of living together as listeners to the Lord had made them excellent listeners to each other, sensitive to each other's feelings. Mary could express Joseph's sorrow, she shared it, she felt it as she felt her own. Jesus could be obedient to them because they were of one mind and one heart.

Joseph, the protector of the child and his mother, died before the savior was crucified for the redemption of mankind. How merciful of the Father in heaven to relieve Joseph of his role as protector before his divine charge was handed over to the executioners. Would it have been possible for Joseph to witness the execution without attempting to prevent it? After all those years of listening to the Lord and following his commands to protect the child from those who wanted to harm him could Joseph have heard a completely new message and stood aside as Jesus was betrayed, tortured, and killed?

Now Mary was asked to give Joseph back to God, to give up this friend, confidante, comforter, protector, for a time. She was asked to go on in the loneliness all widows feel, remembering what once was and feeling somehow incomplete, severed. Only after death would she be reunited with Joseph. Mary was able to give Joseph back to God. If God's plan for her, for Joseph, for Jesus required that Joseph go home to the Father, then that was the greatest good.

Somehow even in Joseph's death, Mary's soul magnified the Lord. Let it be done.

Mary's days as wife were ended, but her role of mother continued. It is in this relationship as mother of Jesus that Mary teaches best.

Mother of the Child Jesus

It is possible to consider Mary's mothering of Jesus in a very limited way. We can acknowledge that she bore him in her womb or served as prenatal incubator and nourisher. Then she birthed him and some conclude her contribution was complete. Much as the decanted infants in Orwell's *1984* severed relationship with the jars in which they gestated prenatally, some see Christ detaching himself from his mother's womb and his mother as well, almost simultaneously.

The fallacy here is that God became man, but not really. God played at being human, being born of woman, but he never was an infant needing the love of a mother for growth, for nourishment, for survival. Nothing could be farther from the truth. There is no untruth in God. He does not pretend to become man or refuse to be fully human. And the relationship which Jesus, God and man had with Mary was fully human.

Whatever is wholesome and real and tender in a mother-child relationship existed between Mary and Jesus. She wrapped him in swaddling clothes and placed him in a manger. She counted his fingers and toes. She studied his eyes until the day she could tell he was able to see. She nursed him and held him and loved him. Later she taught him to speak and delighted in his first words. He learned her accent, her intonation, her idiomatic expressions. She taught him the names of flowers and insects, the words of psalms. Through her, God the Father loved and comforted his Son when he was hurt by bruises or cut by rejection or loneliness. She looked down smiling with pleasure at this child she loved, until one day she found herself looking up into his face. He had grown up.

All these things are very natural. All that is natural in a human life was present in the life of Christ. Mary was the mother chosen by God for the God-man. She was fully a mother and her child was fully human developing from infant to child to adolescent to man.

He did not sit in the dusty road of their little village playing with the other four-year-olds with a consciousness that he was Almighty God participating in this nursery game because that was what little humans did. He sat in the dust with the four-year-olds and he was one of them. How does a four-year-old feel when called a baby by the seven-year-olds? Jesus felt that. How does a five-year-old feel when he loses at a game? Jesus felt that too. How do children learn to bear injustice, pain, rejection? In just those ways Jesus learned what pain and ridicule feel like in the heart, the stomach, and the soul. And he learned that it was good to avoid pain and ridicule whenever possible. He experienced fear and developed courage.

Mary nourished him with love and he developed his gifts to full potential. Some of his talents were inherited from his mother. He bore her genes and they were, quite naturally, determinative of his height, muscular structure, coloring, mental ability, length of eyelashes, and the thousand other human marks uniquely personal to him.

Mary and Joseph taught Jesus his prayers. They took him to temple according to the law and told him about the Lord God of Israel. They witnessed their love of a personal God as they shared their lives with Jesus. He observed them listening to God and learned to assume a listening posture before his Father.

In considering this, one might ask how it was possible for Mary and Joseph to undertake the education of the Messiah, God Incarnate. Would one dare evangelize God? No, but the infant Jesus, the child Jesus needed to be taught, trained, and reared until he reached adulthood and began to realize who he really was.

A common error is to liken the Mary-Jesus relationship to myths and fairy tales in which a trusted nurse (or hunter) is given the royal heir to nurture until such time as it is politically safe to reveal his true identity. The nurse pretends to be the mother of the child. She plays the role, serves the function, provides security, identity and credibility, but she can never be his mother. One day the real parent will return for the child and if the nurse has done her job well, the royal child will be expecting the reunion. In some way, the nurse conveys to the child that she is not the mother, whereas a parent, whether biological or adoptive, conveys the unalterable, permanent relationship of parent to child. One may become angry with one's mother, but she is still mother. A parent may become separated by distance or estranged by opinion from a child. But the child remains son or daughter wherever or however he chooses to live. That is the reality of the life relationship. It is permanent, unbreakable. Mary's relationship to Jesus was the mother relationship. It should not be misconstrued as the nurse relationship. Mary taught as a mother teaches.

One might question how Mary was able to live with the unusual facts regarding her pregnancy and the events surrounding the birth of her child. After the shepherds who came to the manger had adored the infant, they told Mary what the angels had said about the newborn Jesus. Luke tells us, "Mary treasured all these things and reflected on them in her heart." Again on the occasion of their taking the infant to the temple in Jerusalem to present him the Lord, Mary encounters Simeon. Luke describes him as a man who was "just and pious, and awaited the consolation of Israel and the Holy

Spirit was upon him," and further (*Luke 2:26*), "It was revealed to him by the Holy Spirit that he would not experience death until he had seen the Anointed of the Lord." Simeon took Jesus in his arms and thanked God for allowing him to see the Anointed. Then he blessed the family and said to Mary: "This child is destined to be the downfall and the rise of many in Israel, a sign that will be opposed — and you yourself shall be pierced with a sword — so that the thoughts of many hearts may be laid bare." In addition to Simeon's prophecy, Mary and Joseph heard Anna, the prophetess, thanking God and talking about their baby to all who "looked forward to the deliverance of Jerusalem."

How could a young mother hear such an astounding message as Simeon's, "a sign that will be opposed . . . you will be pierced with a sword . . .," or the shepherd's message and continue day-to-day living in a peaceful way? The answer Scripture gives is that Mary kept or treasured all these things, pondering them in her heart.

The words Mary heard were a message from God, a message not completely clear or comprehensible to her. In the seed bed of Mary's heart, nurtured by prayer and reflection, the message could grow and take shape, until one day Mary was able to see, to understand, to perceive that which appeared conflicting to be complementing.

Pondering or keeping in the heart is not a locking away or hiding process, although often those things which are most profound sink and grow within us and are not taken out and shared until later, much later, when they have reached maturity. Pondering in the heart is a prayer-reflection process leading to light and wisdom.

Mary can be a model in handling the impossible in our lives, which will parallel hers. We won't meet Simeon in the temple, but we may listen to a doctor's report: "Your child has a serious disease. By the age of sixteen he will be . . ." At the awareness of death or suffering for self or a loved one, we can scream in agony, weep in rage, demand of God, "Why?" We can also remember Mary and ask her to teach us. "What do I do with this? How could anyone bear this?" The message may be clear enough but the real message, God's plan in all this agony, is not clear. To bring light to the confusion and peace to the chaos in our hearts we need to pray, to reflect. Mary learned that and she can help us, if we are willing to accept that help.

God speaks to man through the circumstances of his life, through a word spoken by a friend, or a stranger encountered significantly. God's message comes in many forms. At times it comes on a wave of joy or good fortune; at other times it arrives in a moment of pain or sorrow. We can accept the joy or good fortune and ignore the giver of the good. We can fail to hear the real message. Or at other times, we can take the problem, obstacle, pain, or sorrow and worry and drag it around endlessly in our minds. We can become so engrossed with the problem and our ability or lack of ability to handle it that we do not seek God in it and fail to hear the message. God, the Merciful One, continues to send messages, opportunities to learn the wisdom he has for us.

In Mary we find a life of listening to the Father and living his Word in her relationships with others. The others, we must remember, were real flesh and blood with the wide spectrum of physical, mental, and spiritual problems we find in our own circle.

If we go to Mary with a problem or a suffering, will she give us worldly wisdom? Will she tell us to cope quietly with the situation, not wearing our hearts on our sleeves, but rather putting up a brave front for the world to see? Will Mary lead us to believe the Christian doesn't need to enjoy life — he only needs to cope with it?

No, Mary is too close to God to believe such things. When called by God she said, "Let it be done," and she said to herself, "Let it be." We hand over to God the impossible call or the problem or the agony or sadness or desperation. We say, "Father, if it is your will, let it be done unto me." And we remember that is passive voice. We are not saying, "I will bring it about; I will do it." We can't say that if it is not truth,

47

but we can say honestly: "There is no way I can fulfill this mission or drink from this cup. But I am willing that it be. You do it in me, Father; I can't do it alone." Then, of course, we must try not to second-guess God. We do not hand over our burden and then take it back again. We let it be, as Mary did. God, the all-caring, knowing, loving Creator who made us and goes on refining, polishing, and perfecting us each day of our lives, says: "Trust me. Please, please trust me." If we can do that, God instills in us peace and joy and love, even for our enemies. And it is real. It is not a pretense, a good front, a pious facade. There is nothing unreal in God. When he brings us through suffering to joy, it is real joy.

Mother of the Man Jesus

No good relationship remains static. As each one grows and develops, the relationship evolves into something deeper. We see Jesus standing in the temple among the teachers. His mother, who is almost thirty years old now, approaches her adolescent son who has been lost for three days and asks why he separated himself from them. She tells him she has been worried.

The answer Jesus gives Mary redefines their relationship. He does not apologize for his absence. Rather, he asks why she has been looking for him so sorrowfully. "Did you not know I had to be in my Father's house?" (*Luke 2:48*). Jesus at the age of twelve refers to God as his Father and seems to be aware that God has called him to a special mission. Sadly, Mary and Joseph did not understand their child, a condition suffered by all parents at some time. Jesus returned home and was "obedient" to them. And it was under their guidance and authority that he continued to grow in wisdom and in grace. Later, perhaps, Mary remembered the words he said in the temple. His life was based on them, and so was hers. Their relationship too was grounded on them.

Mary is not mentioned in Luke's Gospel for several chapters. Jesus prepared for his public ministry by baptism and fasting forty days in the desert. He began preaching and performing miracles. He healed the sick, raised the Widow of Nain's son from the dead, and he forgave sins. "After this he journeyed through towns and villages preaching and proclaiming the good news of the kingdom of God" (*Luke 8:1*). His disciples went with him, as did some women. Three are named: Magdalene; Joanna, who was married to Herod's steward, Chuza; and Susanna. Many others who assisted them "out of their means" are referred to but not named. Mary, the mother of Jesus, is not among them, however.

Consider that two who knew Jesus best were not sent by the Father on his public ministry. John the Baptist knew Jesus. He was stunned when Jesus asked to be baptized by him, certain that it should have been reversed. He complied only after Jesus said to him, "Give in for now. We must do this if we would fulfill all of God's demands" (*Matthew 3:15*). In John's Gospel, the Baptist calls the Lord the Lamb of God and the Anointed One. He releases his disciples to follow Jesus, but he remains at the work God has given him, preaching, calling people to repentance, and baptizing them. John understood: "He must increase, while I must decrease," and "No one can lay hold on anything unless it is given him from on high." Even after John was imprisoned he remained eager to know what Jesus was doing. Again he sent his disciples to him. Finally, John was beheaded by Herod. His mission was complete and he was taken home by the Father. John could certainly attest to the fact that his joy was complete, even though he never received the call to walk with Jesus as did Simon Peter and the other apostles.

Just as John the Baptist was not publicly connected with the ministry of Jesus, neither was Mary.

At one point Mary and other relatives came to meet Jesus. They couldn't get close to him because the crowds were big, but they managed to get a message to him: "Your mother and your brothers are standing outside and they wish to see you." His reply underscores what he said when Joseph and Mary found him in the temple, about twenty years earlier. "My mother and my brothers are those who hear the word of God and act upon it" (*Luke 8:19*). It's possible to look at that statement in one of two ways. One might conclude that Jesus was publicly rejecting his mother and his brethren. Unless one takes the remark out of context, it is difficult to draw that conclusion. In looking at the Mary-Jesus relationship as a continuum we are drawn to another, delightfully astounding conclusion.

Jesus is offering himself as brother to anyone who hears and keeps the Word of God. He invites all men to be one with him, of one family, the children of his Father. He includes himself, his mother, his brethren, and all the rest of "his brethren" throughout time in the same kind of relationship — the unity of those who "hear the word of God and act upon it." Jesus does not reject his family; he broadens it throughout time and place to include all mankind. How happy for us that Jesus loved his mother; he did not idolize her.

Later Jesus tells his friends the conditions of being his disciples. "Whoever wishes to be my follower must deny his very self, take up his cross each day, and follow in my steps. Whoever would save his life will lose it, and whoever loses his life for my sake will save it. What profit does he show who gains the whole world and destroys himself in the process? If a man is ashamed of me and my doctrine, the Son of Man will be ashamed of him when he comes in his glory and that of his Father and his holy angels" (*Luke 9:23-26*).

Mary isn't mentioned here, but Jesus would

51

apply these words to his mother as well as to anyone. Mary's great strength was that she understood living as Jesus taught. He asked all to do whatever was the will of the Father. Her life was given up to that. She had lived almost fifty years and had taken up "the cross" daily if that were God's gift. Jesus repeated the teaching that all who follow him are his brothers and sisters and the children of his Father when the disciples asked him to teach them to pray. He told them to call God "Father" or even "Daddy." Later he gave them a parable showing that earthly fathers give good to their children, concluding that if men who are evil give good to their children, "how much more will the heavenly Father give the Holy Spirit to those who ask him" (*Luke 11:13*).

When a woman in the crowd cried out, as he was teaching, "Blest is the womb that bore you and the breasts that nursed you," Jesus revised the compliment. He didn't deny the statement, but he generalized the condition for happiness or blessedness. "Rather," he replied, "blest are they who hear the word of God and keep it" (*Luke 11:27-28*). Mary is blest because she hears the Word of God and she obeys. Jesus loves and admires his mother not only because she was his mother, but rather because that was God's plan for her and she accepted it. Jesus invites all to be blest. Certainly only one could be his mother. It is equally certain, however, that all could keep the Word of the Father — all could be blest. The

word "blest" is sometimes translated "happy."
Jesus publicly announces that anyone who wants
it can have true happiness. The key to it is hearing
and doing the will of the Father. Mary had the
key, and she used it.

The final hard message Jesus delivered about
family was: "If anyone comes to me without turn-
ing his back on his Father and mother, his wife
and his children, his brothers and sisters, indeed
his very self, he cannot be my Follower. Anyone
who does not take up his cross and follow me
cannot be my disciple." The word "hate" should
be read "be detached from" or "value little", and
there is no doubt that Jesus meant that. Whoever
wanted to follow him would have to detach himself from father, mother, sister, brother, wife and
children, and his very life. He would have to detach himself from his own life and be ready to
drink death like water, as Bishop Fulton Sheen
expressed it.

And if this were meant for anyone who would
follow Christ, it was meant for Mary. She needed
to detach herself, as God called, from parents,
husband, and child. She needed to drink death
like water, if required. And Mary understood that.
She needed that wisdom because only God's truth
could support her in the passion she would share.
There was absolutely no sentimentality in the
Mary-Jesus relationship. Sentimentality and con-
ventionality were worthless. Mary needed the
reality of a God-centered existence.

We come then to the essence of Mary's relationship with Jesus. Mary loved her son. Her love grew through years of caring, sharing, enjoying, understanding. She loved Jesus and she supported him in his mission.

Mary lived God's plan for Mary. She allowed Jesus to live God's plan for Jesus. I am certain there were times she would have liked to be near him during his public ministry, but she was not. It is likely she had concern for his physical needs. Was he eating properly? Was he eating at all? Was he getting enough rest? Was anyone taking care of his clothing? Who were all his new friends? And what of the reports that filtered back to her, reports about the things he was saying about the scribes and Pharisees? Did he have to be so outspoken? Surely he knew he was putting himself into a dangerous position!

If God had wanted Mary with Jesus every day of his mission, she would have gladly been there. If the Father wanted her elsewhere, she would hear his Word and obey it. Mary could trust that her Father would look after her son, providing all he needed.

Mary and Jesus have a God-centered relationship. They love each other; they honor each other; they support each other in doing the Father's will. They never enslave each other. Each of them, Jesus and Mary, look to the Father. They are totally his. Neither would put the other in the position rightfully belonging to the Father alone. Idols were not erected in their hearts.

Understanding this mother-son relationship is

important. We can use it as a model in examining every relationship we have with parents wife, husband, children, brothers, sisters, friends. Is the Lord leading us to consider whether we are capable of detachment? Is every love we have a love that supports the other and helps him do the will of God? Is our love ever possessive? Does it try to hold someone back from that person's mission or ministry? Do we want to be God to someone? If we were to realize we were enslaving those we love, Jesus would say to us what he said to his followers. He required it of himself, his mother, his disciples, and of us. Those who love God, who follow his Son Jesus, will detach themselves from all others, take up their cross, and follow. To paraphrase Goethe, Mary's love did not dominate; it cultivated.

Mother of Mankind

One of the most difficult experiences of life is to watch a loved one suffer and be unable to stop the pain. The prayer, at those moments, is an intercessory scream for help. Cries of "Have pity," "Stop it", "Do something, Lord" reverberate through the brain drowning out all thought. One enters into the suffering, suffers with the other, and cries for deliverance from it.

Anyone who loves experiences this compassion, this suffering with at some time. Mothers experience it with their children. Hearts, prayers, tears are poured out over the hurts, wounds, and fevers of children. Illnesses and accidents are times of powerful intercession, and emergency rooms in hospitals are places for prayer.

A few years ago, I stood over the stretcher of my son, then thirteen, in the corridor of Rhode Island Hospital. Less than an hour earlier he had come to me, his hand trapped in the glass container of the food blender, his finger pierced through and impaled on the blade, and blood running up his arm. Wrapping his wrist in towels so broken glass wouldn't puncture a vein, I smashed the glass container with a hammer and freed his finger from the blade. He was bleeding heavily and we rushed him to the hospital. He lay there bleeding on a stretcher, his hand wrapped in gauze, waiting for a doctor.

As I stood next to the stretcher in the busy hospital corridor, a thought filled me completely. When Jesus was bleeding, no one was coming to help him.

I was weeping. I was standing weeping over the stretcher because my child was in pain. I felt his pain. Then I thought of Mary.

Her child, from the time he was arrested until the time he died, was covered with bruises, cuts, sores, wounds, and welts. He was humiliated in every way. He was spat upon and degraded. Mary followed him along the way of the cross, and she felt his pain. Her heart, as Simeon prophesied, was pierced. *Mater Dolorosa,*

Mother of Sorrows. She watched him tortured, spilling his blood in the gutters of Jerusalem. And she accepted it all. "Father, may your will be done in this." If she had not agreed to this crucifixion, she would have died on the road to Calvary. She could not have survived seeing the Son of the Most High tormented so.

Mary did agree because she had spent fifty years learning that "Blessed is he who does the will of my Father." She agreed. At the moment she said yes to the way of the cross, yes to the falling and spitting and beating, at the moment she said, "Father, may your will be done — I accept this horror," at that moment Mary became the mother of mankind. She agreed to the redemption. She gave her son. She let him go, carrying his cross, and she accepted the Father's plan. Mary, the mother of the Redeemer, became the mother of the redeemed. She became the mother of all mankind.

Mother of the Church

Finally, we see Mary standing at the foot of the cross with her sister and the beloved disciple. Jesus speaks to his mother. "Woman, here is your son." Then he speaks to the disciple, "Here is your mother." From that time the disciple took care of Mary, as a son would his mother. Jesus, dying of asphyxiation on the cross, gasped out his words. He wanted to provide for his widowed mother.

When he called her Woman, he named her the new Eve, the new mother of God's children. Just as he was the new Adam, she was the new mother, the mother of the redemption. Mary had accepted the crucifixion of her son on the way to Calvary. What was the impact of his words now?

Standing at the foot of the cross, utterly spent, in agony, Mary is an empty vessel and the Spirit is praying in her. Then Jesus speaks giving her a new command, a new call, "Woman, this is your son," and down through the years Mary's heart echoes, "I am the handmaid of the Lord. Let what you say be done." She agrees to go on living. She will not die no matter how much she craves to go home to her Father, to her husband, Joseph, and to be reunited with her dying son. She will live, because that is the will of her Father.

The infant Church needed her. We are told she lived about twenty-five years after Jesus died and rose. The Church was a quarter of a century old before the mother of the Church was called to go home to her Father's house.

What Is Her Name?

One day during an eight-day silent retreat at the Diocesan Spiritual Life Center in Pawtucket, Rhode Island, we retreatants were asked by Sr. Kieran Flynn, R.S.M., who was directing our retreat, to be with Jesus as he went to his mother after the resurrection.

Pawtucket is a small New England city with urban blight and urban renewal, with choice neighborhoods and run-down areas. The Spiritual Life Center is on Power Road, surrounded by modest homes centered on small plots of ground. There is an excellent place for long walks, however, in St. Francis Cemetery across Smithfield Pike.

Throughout the retreat we went in single file with our Bibles and notebooks, fanning out along the drives and paths of the cemetery, resting on gravestones, weeding a bit, reading, meditating, walking and engaged — completely, totally engaged — in conversation with God, who was graciously present.

This particular morning as I walked through the great iron gates and made a left turn on the first drive after a huge Art Nouveau angel, I began thinking of Mary.

Jesus had been taken down from the cross and buried on Friday evening. All day Saturday Mary lived on faith. She knew that Jesus would do what he said he would do. But how was that possible now? Jesus was dead. He was brutally killed and he was buried. Faith kept her alive, but she was in agony still. Jesus was in the tomb and she suffered all day Saturday.

Then Jesus rose. We don't see it in Scripture, but we know that when he rose, Jesus went to see his mother.

Walking along the northern tier of the cemetery, I was thinking of Jesus, the risen Lord. His body had been in such agony before he died. Now he was back and all the wounds were transformed into glory. He was revelling in the glory of God's earth, his Father's earth, a redeemed planet. For the first time, he walked on the redeemed planet Earth. It had been done. It was accomplished.

It wasn't possible to walk. I needed to run, to skip, to leap, to throw back my head smiling into the warmth of the sun, to smell the grass, to watch each cloud formation, to bless the Father for all the beauty of the earth.

And then Jesus went to his mother. How did he feel? What did he feel as he approached her? I stopped suddenly under a horse chestnut tree. I could not move. As I stood there immobile, the question surged through me, "What did he call her?" The answer was vital. I knew that until I had that answered I would not be able to move, to take another step.

Jesus came upon her. She didn't know he was coming. She was drained and in great sorrow. He entered the house and spoke to her. What did he call her? Did he say Mary, woman, mother, child, daughter, sister? What did he call her?

Finally, I knew. He called her mother. He had to call her mother, because she had become the universal, eternal mother. Just as she waited patiently while he came through the crucifixion into the resurrection, so too she would wait for each one of us, because she had accepted the role of mother of mankind. She did not suffer the cross, she accepted it. She allowed me to be redeemed. she became my mother. And what she did for Jesus in his passion, she does for me in mine.

Whenever there is pain or suffering, danger or trouble, she is there praying, loving, supporting. Mary is one who is always there whenever you need her. She can be trusted. She can be relied upon. And that, after all, is the Model Relative.

Along the Gathering Stream
A Story

Mary, the Suffering Servant
Sharyn Malloy

"For the Son of Man himself did not come to be served but to serve, and to give his life as a ransom for many" (Mark. 10:45)*. This is a passage familiar to most of us and particularly cherished because it speaks of the suffering of the Lord on our behalf. Here he names himself as the Son of Man, which is an Old Testament title for a great personage who would come bearing the authority of the Almighty. However, he says that he, as this Son of Man, is first of all a servant. He didn't come to receive honors or service for himself, but rather to give service and that consisting particularly of a kind of sacrificial living and dying for others.

Living with the mystery of Christ's passion and death, day in and day out, we have become accustomed to this idea and are almost immune to the shock effect it had originally. In Mark

*All scriptural quotations will be taken from *The Jerusalem Bible*, Garden City, New York: Doubleday and Company, Inc., 1966.

8:31, where Jesus first expresses this notion to his disciples, we get some sense of the impact that it bore:

> And he began to teach them that the Son of Man was destined to suffer grievously, to be rejected by the elders and the chief priests and the scribes, and to be put to death, and after three days to rise again; and he said all this quite openly. Then, taking him aside, Peter started to remonstrate with him. But, turning and seeing his disciples, he rebuked Peter and said to him, "Get behind me, Satan! Because the way you think is not God's way but man's."

We often think that Peter was so taken aback in this passage because it distressed him to think of his beloved friend having to suffer. I believe that that is so, but there is also another element present which usually we do not take into account. That is the element of the shock to the Jewish mind of what Jesus is saying at this time. Jesus calls himself "the Son of Man" and yet he says that his Son of Man has to suffer. Peter, as the typical Jew of his day, never heard of such a thing! Why is that? It is because this is the very first time in the history of scriptural interpretation that these particular ideas are joined! Jesus joins them to express the fullness of who he is and why he came. This strikes Peter as so foreign to all that he knows and understands that he almost cannot accept it. Let's take a look at those two separate ideas joined in one.

By the time Jesus walked the earth, the Jews held certain fixed concepts concerning this Son of Man about whom they read in Daniel 7:13f:

I gazed into the visions of the night.
And I saw, coming on the clouds of heaven,
one like a son of man.
He came to the one of great age
and was led into his presence.
On him was conferred sovereignty,
glory and kingship,
and men of all peoples, nations and lan-
    guages became his servants.
His sovereignty is an eternal sovereignty
which shall never pass away,
nor will his empire ever be destroyed.

This was a marvelous prophecy for Jesus' compatriots particularly because they were under Roman domination, humbled, without authority, without self-government, without freedom. These words in Daniel assured them that this Son of Man would someday come to put the Romans in their place and exalt Israel, giving Israel the rule. Not only that, but Israel would also be made to rule over the other nations as well, with a sovereignty that insurrec- tions or the assault of foreign powers could not end.

As we notice, there are no hints of suffering

whatsoever here: just one quick victory and the reign belongs to Israel! Thus we see that the Son of Man became for the Jews a figure of glory and the incarnation of God's triumph on behalf of his chosen people.

Now there was also another set of passages, often the subject of meditation and prayer, which held forth a mysterious "servant of the Lord" whose very suffering seemed to be his service to the Lord. The Jews were hard put to find out exactly who this suffering servant was. We can understand something of their confusion and their puzzlement by looking at Acts 8:27ff:

Now it happened that an Ethiopian had been on pilgrimage to Jerusalem; he was a eunuch and an officer at the court of the . . . queen, of Ethiopia. . . . He was now on his way home; and as he sat in his chariot he was reading the prophet Isaiah. The Spirit said to Phillip, "Go up and meet that chariot." When Philip ran up, he heard him reading Isaiah the prophet and asked, "Do you understand what you are reading?" "How can I," he replied, "unless I have someone to guide me?" So he invited Philip to get in and sit by his side. Now the passage of scripture he was reading was this:

   "Like a sheep that is led to the slaughter-
        house,
   like a lamb that is dumb in front of its

shearers,
like these he never opens his mouth.
He has been humiliated and has no one to
defend him.
Who will ever talk about his descendants,
since his life on earth has been cut short!"
The eunuch turned to Philip and said, "Tell
me, is the prophet referring to himself or
someone else?" Starting, therefore, with
this text of scripture Philip proceeded to
explain the Good News of Jesus to him.

The text that Philip used is an excerpt from a
larger passage which goes into detail about the
sufferings of this servant of the Lord. We can see
from the eunuch's question to Philip that he,
like the Jews of the time, was plainly in great
puzzlement and confusion as to the identity of
this mysterious servant.

Now Jesus, much to the dismay and shock of
his contemporaries, joined the passage just
quoted from Isaiah with that about the glorious
Son of Man, coming in power and majesty to
receive eternal sovereignty. His purpose was to
point out that the Son of Man is also the
suffering servant and that he will come into his
kingdom only by his sufferings. What a blow!
This was intolerable! We can now better understand Peter's reaction: "Heaven preserve you,
Lord; . . . this must not happen to you" (*Matthew 16:22*). Jesus was the Son of Man; the
suffering servant was an entirely different thing!

Jesus pressed his point and said, "Peter, the way you think is not God's way but man's." Jesus, in that moment, totally revolutionized the thinking about those two passages so central in Jewish spirituality and life.

However, was Jesus himself totally able to accept the destiny that he described here? Because we know that he died in the manner that his Father had prescribed for him and that he rose again, which is his Father's approval of him, we can conclude that he did embrace the destiny which he foretold would be his. Before that, however, Jesus had to struggle with the very concepts that he was laying out. He had to struggle with the fact that the Son of Man had to be the suffering servant also. In Mark 14:33b-35 we can sense something of this ordeal as we see him in the garden of Gethsemane:

> And a sudden fear came over him, and great distress. And he said to them, "My soul is sorrowful to the point of death. Wait here, and keep awake." And going on a little further he threw himself on the ground and prayed that, if it were possible, this hour might pass him by.

He prays so poignantly, "Abba (Father)! . . . Everything is possible for you. Take this cup away from me. But let it be as you, not I, would have it." Jesus, coming to the very last hours of his life on earth, was still struggling to embrace fully the fact that, as the Son of Man destined for glory and everlasting sovereignty, he would come into his kingdom only through the bitterest of suffering. While Jesus never retracted the yes that he had given to the Father, he did have his own human emotions and feelings to deal with, which places him squarely in a position of identification with us.

As we might suspect, then, this struggle did not end with Jesus. One of the very purposes for Mark's Gospel was to encourage the Christians of Rome to accept the fact that they too had become the suffering servants of Yahweh, just like Jesus. Although it was with great difficulty that they accepted the crucified Jesus as the Messiah, it was with even greater struggle that they wrestled with their own call to take up the cross and follow after Jesus. Jesus was triumphant in glory now. Why should they, his followers, have to repeat in their own lives the same humiliation and dying? This was the hard blow for the Roman community. Was it not just a few years before that Paul himself reasoned with them in a letter, speaking about the very same point?

You have been taught that when we were baptized in Christ Jesus we were baptized in his death; in other words, when we were baptized we went into the tomb with him and joined him in death, so that as Christ was raised from the dead by the Father's glory, we too might live a new life. . . . We must realise that our former selves have been crucified with him to destroy this sinful body and to free us from the slavery of sin . . . you too must consider yourselves to be dead to sin but alive for God in Christ Jesus *(Romans 6 passim).*

The Roman Christians, then, and all Christians since have had to come to terms with the call to share in the ministry of the suffering servant of the Lord. However, I would like to leave that scene for a moment. We will come back to deal with our own feelings on that matter in a while.

Let's turn to Mary now. As the mirror of Jesus and the model of the Church, was she preserved from this struggle? How did she face this question? Perhaps we can look to Luke, the author of that two-volume work of the Gospel and the Acts of the Apostles, for some sense of how Mary dealt with this mystery. He is writing with fifty years of meditation on the mysteries of Jesus behind him, fifty years of insight. In the very first chapter of his Gospel he presents Mary to us. Although this passage is very familiar to us, perhaps we could look at it in a slightly different light, remembering that Luke was most probably a medical man, gifted with deep psychological insight. So we will see Mary having to come to grips with the call of the Lord. This passage is filled with emotional overtones, with struggle, with process. Let's see now how Mary experiences the announcement from the angel of the Lord.

The angel comes in and, quite characteristically, he says, "Rejoice, so highly favoured! The Lord is with you." What is her reaction? She was deeply disturbed by these words. The first encounter with God breaking into her life in a new way caused her deep disturbance. She asked herself what this greeting could mean. Here were darkness and mystery where we have normally expected light, candles, flowers and glory! The angel now begins to enter into a relationship with her to help her come to a place where she can give her full yes. He says to her, "Mary, do not be afraid. . . . We know that this is one of the characteristic things angels say both in the Old and New Testaments. I think that there is some basis for it here. To reassure her, the angel continues, "You have won God's favour. Listen! You are to conceive and bear a son, and you must name him Jesus. He will be great and will be called Son of the Most High. The Lord God will give him the throne of his ancestor David; he will rule over the House of Jacob forever and his reign will have no end." Now we could easily think that that would settle the matter. Not at all! Look at Mary's retort. Mary said to the angel, "But how can this come about, since I am a virgin?" A legitimate question, but still a question! There is darkness as to the means, a wanting to find out a little bit more before the commitment, even though the commitment is forthcoming. The angel has to help her even more. He reaches down deeply into her soul to help her open up to the will of God for her life — an opening up to mystery and darkness. "The Holy Spirit will come upon you," the angel answered, "and the power of the Most High will cover you with its shadow. And so the child will be holy and will be called Son of God." Now even though the angel points out the child's intimate association with the divinity, he desires to give her even more assurance, so he extends to her a sign: "Know this too: your kinswoman Elizabeth has, in her old age, herself conceived a son, and she whom people called barren is now in her sixth month. . . ." That is rather large assurance! However, the angel goes on to say the last word to her that will just make the difference between "I don't know" and "Yes": ". . . for nothing is impossible to God." This is the point where she can give her wholehearted yes. "I am the handmaid of the Lord," said Mary. "Let what you have said be done to me." The angel then left her.

Now notice what Mary said. She identifies herself in this process as a servant. Whether or not she is aware of it at this moment, she's beginning to enter into the whole mystery of being joined to Jesus' life and, in a special way, to the suffering of that life. She, in her turn, becomes the suffering servant. She has given her first commitment, and, I dare say, her final, since the Lord never has to ask her again. She

73

has given it once for all. However, just like Jesus, she had to grow into being able to embrace that call of God in her life. We shall now look at that.

As we consider Mary's early days with Jesus, we get a sense of how filled with mystery they were. She was led here and there, not knowing exactly what to do but always trusting. As we move to the scene of the presentation in the temple (*Luke 2:22-38*), our sense of this mystery becomes clearer: now we see both Mary and Jesus identified as having a ministry of suffering for others!

> As the child's father and mother stood there wondering at the things that were being said about him, Simeon blessed them and said to Mary his mother, "You see this child: he is destined for the fall and for the rising of many in Israel, destined to be a sign that is rejected."

What does this mean? Perhaps we can get some idea in the very next announcement: ". . . and a sword will pierce your own soul too. . . ." That word "too" is pregnant with significance, for it means that Jesus has been given a ministry of suffering in which Mary would share with full participation. All of this would be "so that the secret thoughts of many may be laid bare."

When you get an announcement like that, what do you do with it? When you are told that your whole life and the life of the one you most dearly cherish will be a life of suffering for the benefit of others, what do you do? Well, you probably do what Mary did: "His mother stored up all these things in her heart" (*Luke 2:51*). This is not the storing up as of mementos, but rather the active process of cherishing the things that are stored up, cherishing and dealing with them. Mary had to deal with the fact that this son of hers, conceived in glory and destined for glory, would suffer rejection and death at the hands of his people. Not only would she have to witness that, but she would share in his experience as well.

Now, do we have any other indications in the rest of the Gospel of how Mary handled this burden that was hers? Strangely enough, Luke hardly says another word about Mary. There are only a few other references, slight indeed, which indicated that he sees Mary as a listener whom we are to imitate, a listener to God's Word (*cf. Luke 8:21*). This is the end of what Luke presents to us about Mary, in his Gospel. Personally, I think that this silence is full. What do you do, anyway, when you have been given an announcement like the one we just read? You deal with it, for years and years. You work it over and over with each new suffering, with each new trial, with each new blow, with each new situation in which your beloved son or daughter or friend, your goods, your life, or whatever you hold dear is torn from you and destroyed. You deal with it, wondering, questioning, seeking:

Why, God? What does this mean? Abba, everything is possible to you. Take this cup away from me, yet, not my will but yours be done.

Perhaps we can glean yet one more hint of Mary from *Luke 21:1-4* which, while it does not refer to Mary, contains reverberations of her spirit in the heart of Jesus. The scene takes place a few days before Jesus goes to his death.

> As he looked up he saw rich people putting their offerings into the treasury; then he happened to notice a poverty-stricken widow putting in two small coins, and he said, "I tell you truly, this poor widow has put in more than any of them; for these have all contributed money they had over, but she from the little she had has put in all she had to live on."

Scholars agree that Jesus sees in this little scene a premonition of his own death. He is like the poor woman who has given all she has to live on. Were thoughts of his mother, also a widow, in his heart at this time? With the death of her son, she would truly have given up all that she had to live on. Jesus was her life. So we see Mary still dealing here with her call, and the cross is still ahead.

The next and final time that Luke mentions Mary is in his other volume, the Acts of the Apostles. The scene here is very different from what we have just been considering. We know

the scene: it's just before Pentecost. In Acts
1:14, we read: "All these [i.e., the apostles]
joined in continuous prayer, together with several women, including Mary the mother of Jesus,
and with his brothers." This final time that we
see her, she is set aside as very special. It appears
that she has successfully dealt with the question
of whether or not she could be for Yahweh the
suffering servant. How do we know this? Let's
look at Isaiah 53, which is the song of the
Suffering Servant of Yahweh. As we read, we
will see how Mary receives the promise contained therein, the promise made only to the
one who accepts the role of the suffering servant
and lives it through to the end. Beginning with
verse 10, we shall read this as if it referred to
Mary:

> Yahweh has been pleased to crush her with
>   suffering.
> If she offers her life in atonement,
> she shall see her heirs, she shall have a long
>   life
> and through her what Yahweh wishes will
>   be done.

The truth of this is evident after Pentecost. For,
in giving up one son, she has gained many sons
and daughters.

> Her soul's anguish over
> she shall see the light and be content.

By her sufferings shall my servant justify
  many,
taking their faults on herself.

Here we remember the prophecy of Simeon:
". . . and a sword will pierce your own soul too
— so that the secret thoughts of many may be
laid bare."

Hence I will grant whole hordes for her
  tribute,
she shall divide the spoil with the mighty,
for surrendering herself to death
and letting herself be taken for a sinner
while she was bearing the faults of many
and praying all the time for sinners.

This is the stance we see her take at Pentecost
when, in the midst of the people her son has
gained for the Father, she receives her share of
the outpouring of the Spirit, as she continued in
prayer with them and for them.

So we see that Mary, somehow, was able to
deal with God's call to her to share in the
sufferings of her son, the Servant of Yahweh.
Despite all the glory that was promised, she had
to go through the suffering first. In this time
when so many are not only suffering but
struggling with the very idea of having to suffer,
I would like to suggest that Mary is one who
would help us to come through to the place that
she came to, that she would help us to receive

the fulfillment of the promise that she herself has received. She will help us to say yes. She will teach us to be disciples, suffering servants, according to the pattern of Jesus because, just as it says at the very end of Isaiah 53, she is praying all the time for us sinners.

Living Under the Glory Spout
John Randall, S.T.D.

I'd like to share some insights into Christian living that the Lord gave me following a weekend renewal conference. There is power present at charismatic conferences — healings galore, beautiful praise, healed relationships, and people aglow. We are reminded of Pentecostal leader Bob Mumford's image of the Glory Spout: when we are under the Glory Spout, God's glory pours down on us and it seems as though nothing can go wrong. It's a sunny day and joy, peace, power and love are everywhere.

After the conference, I felt that the Lord was saying, "Jake, you know that Glory Spout you experienced at that conference? You can be under it always." I said, "Do you mean that, Lord?" He said, "Yes, the secret is this: go to my mother and she will show you how to stay under the Glory Spout. Ever since I rose from the dead, the heavens have been open. My Spirit is being poured out. The Glory Spout is on. I haven't turned it off. I want you to live in the fullness of my resurrection, and my mother will show you how. The problem is this. My glory is always being poured out. Sometimes at a retreat, at a conference or high moments of grace, you are directly under the spout and in the light." "However," the Lord continued, "what happens is that you drift away from the spot and need to be drawn back under the Glory Spout. I haven't moved — you have," the Lord said.

This is a little like a young married couple driving a car. They seem to be driving the car together. A few years later, they've moved apart. The wife is over near the door as if she is trying to get out of the car. And she says to her husband, "What's happened, dear? We aren't as close as we used to be." And he answers, "But I haven't moved." Something similar happens to us. God doesn't move. His Glory Spout is on. His wisdom, his Word, his power, his healing, his goodness, his abundant life, and his resurrection power are constantly being poured out on us. But we drift away.

Let's look at another image that may help us. I used to have an old FM radio tuner that had what I would call a drifting dial. When I tuned in a station the reception was clear at first, but five or ten minutes later, the music became fuzzy. Somehow or other the dial would drift and I'd have to come back to the set, put it on the exact spot, and then the music would come forth clear as a bell again. We are very much like that drifting dial. Somehow or other, we are pulled away by a centrifugal force: the forces of Satan, the world, and the flesh. And we say, "Where are you, Lord? Where have you gone? How come I'm in the darkness?" And the Lord says, "I'm over here; come back." I would like to share the secret of remaining under the Glory Spout.

Mary is called the "Seat of Wisdom." This title reminds me of a statue of Mary I saw in the halls of the University of Louvain. Here was Mary, a young girl who never went to high school or college, portrayed as the Seat of Wisdom and hence the patroness of learning. Of course, this shouldn't be too astounding. Remember Jesus said, "Father, I give you thanks that you have hidden these things from the wise and the clever and revealed them to little ones. Yes, Father, such was thy pleasure."

Mary is called the Seat of Wisdom because she was attuned to God. The Holy Spirit was poured into her so fully that the Son of God took flesh in her womb. She became pregnant with God and gave him to the world, conceiving him, as Augustine said, in her mind before her flesh. Thus we call her "the Seat of Wisdom." And what the Lord said was, "You, too, can be and should be a seat of wisdom. I want you all to be seats of wisdom. If you are under the Glory Spout and never move away from it, you will be absorbing my wisdom all the time. This is what I want for you — look to my mother and learn. At times it was not easy for her to stay under the Glory Spout. She literally stood at the foot of the cross, clinging to it, a sword in her heart. But nonetheless, even when the apostles had run away and everyone else had run away, she was still there, a nondrifting dial, clinging to the cross. My life was still pouring into her and she was still saying yes. Now, in times of trial like that, in order to be a seat of wisdom, you have to put your arms around the cross and cling to it as if to a raft in swirling waters. As you cling to the cross, you will remain under the Glory Spout. The centrifugal forces present during testing and trials will not take you away and you will have quick victory, quick resurrection."

In this regard, besides Mary, the Mother of God, there are other illustrations. Mother Basilea Schlink, the famous evangelical German nun who writes so beautifully about miraculous living, about bridal love, about always being in tune with the Holy Spirit, about kingdom living, about having the Lord in a daily way, to speak and act and heal and build up a whole new world, is another example. You might say that Basilea Schlink is a seat of wisdom, one who has learned the secret of staying under the Glory Spout, always tuned with a nondrifting dial. Or we can look at the deceased evangelist Kathryn Kuhlman, through whom the Lord worked so many miracles of healing. Once she was asked, "How do you prepare for these healing services?" And she answered, "I don't. I have to stay prepared." What she was saying was, "I always have to be in union with the Lord. I dream of the Lord. "I think upon him,' as the psalmist said, 'on my couch at night.' I'm always in tune with him. I try to keep the great commandment which is to love the Lord with your whole heart, and your whole soul, and your whole mind, and your whole strength."

One who loves the Lord is always thinking of him. His name is magic. St. Francis of Assisi lived that way. He once said he never had to prepare a sermon. His mind was always on the Lord. They — Francis, Basilea Schlink, Kathryn Kuhlman — were all seats of wisdom with nondrifting dials. Eating, drinking and sleeping Jesus, their lives were fixed on him.

For example, when Kathryn Kuhlman was at a healing service and she knew that someone was being healed in the balcony or in the lower left side of the hall, or in the rear, she knew God was healing because she was in a state of bridal love with Jesus, the bridegroom who does all the healing. Because she was the bride and the bridegroom tells the bride everything, it was as if she were constantly hearing, "Look, I'm doing something over here. I'm healing this cancer over here; I'm raising my cripple down there." And the bride, because she was so in tune with the bridegroom, had that power and wisdom streaming into her and she was a seat of wisdom.

The power of the Lord is flowing. The secret of power in Christianity is bridal love. We often think that power in Christianity is being manly, being the bridegroom. This is not so. If you read the Scriptures carefully, the secret of Christianity is in the figure of the bride. It's Jesus who has the muscle, who has the wisdom. He alone is our righteousness. As we love him with a bridal love, with a Mary-type love, with a Basilea Schlink or Kathryn Kuhlman love, we become seats of wisdom. We become the bride to whom the bridegroom tells everything. The power of the Lord is released into the world in a constant way. We can always be under the Glory Spout. The problem with us is that not only do we drift away with the centrifugal forces and trials and testing, but when we drift away we drag others with us. Sometimes even as a whole community we move thirty or forty degrees from the Glory Spout. We say, "Lord, where are you? What's happening? What's happening to this community?" The Lord answers, "I'm still here. My Glory Spout is still on. Why did you drift away?" The constant refrain from Scriptures is "Come back, come back, virgin Israel. I am still your bridegroom."

Think of a compass needle. A compass needle, no matter what happens, always points north. If we could be like that compass needle, our eyes would always be fixed on Jesus, not letting Satan or anyone else distract us from that focus on Jesus which we can always have. Just as the compass needle is drawn to the north, our eyes should be fixed on Jesus.

In each of our lives, the Lord puts us under the Glory Spout, and then he says to us, "Now do you think you can stay there?" We say, "Absolutely, Lord; I've got my bucket of glory. I've just come through this retreat; I've been filled with the Spirit in a new kind of way. I'm all set." The Lord says, "Well, let's see. I'm going to test you and see whether you can stay under the Glory Spout."

What is God's purpose in testing us? I'd like to quote a passage from the fourth chapter of Sirach (Sirach 4:16-18). The Lord talks to us about wisdom. "If one trusts her, he will possess her; his descendants too will inherit her." Here's the rub now: "She walks with him as a stranger, and at first she puts him to the test; fear and dread she brings upon him and tries him with her discipline; with her precepts she puts him to the proof, until his heart is fully with her." There is the key line. The Lord tests us until our hearts are fully with him. He walks with us as a stranger until through our yearning we realize he hasn't left us. We're tested. We're loving him for himself, not for the gifts he may give us. Our love is being purified.

Now, when we pass that test, when we have clung to the cross through trials and difficulties with the forces of Satan and the world and the flesh, when our hearts are fully with the Lord, wisdom returns. Scripture says, "Then she comes back to bring him happiness and reveal her secrets to him." God, the bridegroom, will reveal his deepest secrets to the bride. Jesus said, "I have made known to you all that I heard from my Father" (*John 15:15*). Through the prophet Amos we learn that "The Lord God does nothing without revealing his plan to his servants, the prophets" (*Amos 3:7*). It was said of Elisha that he knew what was happening in the king's bedroom (*2 Kings 6:12*). Elisha was the Lord's man. He was under the Glory Spout, and so the Lord was able to work powerful miracles through him.

Sirach, chapter 4, ends, "But if he fails her" — if he drifts away from the Glory Spout — when the test comes "she will abandon him and deliver him into the hands of despoilers."

The Lord will not entrust to us his real riches, his real secrets, his real wisdom, his real miracles, until he can trust us. As Jesus said, "Do not give what is holy to dogs or toss your pearls before swine" (*Matthew 7:6*). This is a very important line of the New Testament that we often gloss over. But when we've been tested, when we've been pruned, we become a seat of wisdom. A strong person anchored to the foot of the cross has the glory of God, the wisdom of God pouring down into him. When we have passed that test, God reveals his deepest secrets to us. He lets us know everything. We are the bride who leans on the beloved and who receives from the bridegroom all his love, his life, his joy, his peace, his wisdom. You see, God is always speaking. He is never silent. The problem is we are closed. Our ears are closed. Our eyes are closed. Our minds are not on Jesus. That is why the monks of the East, for example, always try to say the Jesus Prayer so that their minds are always on Jesus. And if our minds are always on Jesus, we can have a constantly tuned-in radio. We can know what he is doing. The excitement is there; we have the joy of this contemplative union with the Lord. The Lord says, "Ephpha-tha." Our ears and our eyes are opened to what he is doing and we hear him. This is Glory Spout living and this is what the Lord wants for us all, by virtue of his resurrection. The heavens are open in the Christian dispensation. If we are not under that open heaven, it is our doing.

Bob Mumford gave a beautiful teaching on the principles of temptation in which he talked about the four P's. These four steps are the Promise, the Principle, the Problem and the Provision. First of all God gives us a promise. He gives us, in this case, the promise of Glory Spout living. Then he gives us the principle, the secret of staying under the Glory Spout, of not drifting nor letting anything distract us. We must keep our eyes on Jesus, no matter what. The Lord says, "I'm going to test you; I'm going to walk with you as a stranger, but I'm never going to be away from you. I may be as a stranger to you but I'll be at your side. Remember that. Even though it may seem as if I'm a thousand miles away from you, I'll always be with you. Hang in there; hang on to the cross. Then I send you the problem, a test. If you weather that test, if you keep praising me, if you don't moan and complain and groan, if you stay there, faithful like my mother at the foot of the cross, you will soon see the victory. You will have a quick resurrection. You will come into the provision, the fourth *P* of the promise that I gave to you." "Many people receive buckets and buckets of promises but never come into the provision," Mumford says, "because they haven't really grasped the teaching. They say to the Lord, 'Yes, I grasp that, Lord; ready to go.' But when the Lord sends the problem, the test, they fail. They scream, 'Lord, where are you?' like the Israelites in the desert, who moaned, murmured and complained when the Lord sent saraph serpents to them to bring them back. They had forgotten that the Lord was with them every moment. They were not passing the test." They did not believe in God's constant bridal love for them.

Do you believe that God wants you under the Glory Spout at all times? This is an important question. Do you believe that you can even dream about Jesus like the psalmist, that you can think about him even on your couch? Do you pray that your mind will always be fixed on Jesus, like the compass needle pointing to the north? Do you believe that God wants this for you? He does. He says very explicitly in the Scriptures that he wants this Glory Spout living for us. We need to believe that. The only way to attain this is to hang on to the cross and not let ourselves be pushed about like the reed Jesus speaks of in the case of John the Baptist. He said, "What did you go out to see in the desert — a reed swayed by the wind?" (*Luke 7:24*). No. He implied that John was an oak. He was a seat of wisdom. He was one who didn't drift but stood, like Mary, hanging on to the cross.

Let's take a look at a few more examples from Scripture concerning Glory Spout living. During the Easter season there are some beautiful accounts of quick resurrection victories. Stephen, for example, knew the risen Lord Jesus. He knew the Apostles, and he had often tasted the glory of the Lord. But Stephen underwent a trial similar to that of Jesus. He was brought before the Sanhedrin and falsely accused; everybody abandoned him and he was stoned. But Scripture says that Stephen looked up in the midst of the flying stones and false accusations; he gazed into the heavens and saw Jesus. As he was stoned to death, he had his eyes on him and forgave his enemies because he saw Jesus doing that. Stephen experienced a quick resurrection. Saul was one of the enemies stoning him. Stephen prayed for Saul as Jesus prayed for the good thief on the cross. Within a day or two, Saul was converted and became an evangelist many times more powerful than Stephen might have been.

Then again we have Peter and John thrown into jail after they cured the man at the temple gate in the name of Jesus. Thrown into jail, they rejoiced that they could suffer like their Master.

The community prayed and an angel of the Lord delivered them that very night. The gates of the prison were opened and out they went. The next day they went out preaching the name of Jesus again. They didn't care whether they lived or died. They stood under the Glory Spout and the Lord performed miracle after miracle. People wanted to stand in Peter's shadow so they would be cured, because he was a glory spout. Peter was a glory spout because he was under God's glory and the power of the Lord was streaming through him. Paul and Philip were the same in the early Church. The victory of the resurrection was constantly emanating from them.

An even better example was Paul and Silas. This is one of my favorite examples of the Glory Spout. They had just received in prayer a message from the Holy Spirit that they were to leave Asia and go into Macedonia. They had a vision in the night. A Macedonian appeared to Paul calling, "Come over here." So they abandoned their previous plans, went into Macedonia and brought the Gospel there for the first time as a result of this vision. They went into Philippi and very successfully began an initiation of Philippi into the kingdom of God by working miracles. In the process of doing this, Paul cast out a spirit of divination in a young girl who was fortune telling. Her masters became angry and Paul was thrown into jail with Silas. They were beaten without a trial because they were foreigners. Beaten and bloody, they were put in the stocks in the pit of the jail at night. It looked like their mission was a fiasco. Now what happened to Paul and Silas? Were they murmuring, complaining, saying, "Where are you, Lord?" Did Silas say to Paul, "Are you sure about your guidance? Are you sure the Holy Spirit led us here?" No, they weren't murmuring; they weren't complaining. We read in Acts 16 that Paul and Silas, bloodied and beaten, were singing hymns and praising God at midnight to the astonishment of the jailer and the other prisoners. Crazy Christianity!

What happened? The Lord sent an earthquake, opened the jail right up, and converted the jailer and the whole town. Thus Philippi, one of Paul's favorite communities, was won and the evangelization of Macedonia was begun. As we learn to stay under the Glory Spout, to praise God, to pray to him with thanksgiving in our hearts, we can experience quick resurrections. We can come to know the power and wisdom of the Lord. We can come to be glory spouts ourselves over and over again.

The heart of all religion, Jesus said, is the great commandment which sums up the whole Law and the prophets, the whole Bible, namely, that we love the Lord with our whole heart, our whole strength and our whole mind and that we love our neighbor as ourselves.

This greatest commandment calls us to a bridal love, wherein we become as totally absorbed with the Lord as Mary was. Jesus was her son and her God, and so he was always on her mind. She is the perfect model for us. Our purpose in life is to love the Lord as Mary did — not to be drifting dials but to have our eyes always on Jesus and what he is doing, to live for his glory and for his praise. When we have that kind of love, we are never separated from the Lord.

We have some everyday examples of this kind of love. Consider a mother's love for her baby. Because she loves her baby, she will hear it cry in the night when no one else will. It is as if there is a glory spout between the mother and the child. She will hear that baby's voice in a crowd. It is the same with a lover and the beloved. A lover will hear the beloved's voice in a crowd when no one else will. Why? Because of love, the great commandment, if you will. One is in love; one hears. Love hears; love has ears.

When we realize that we're meant to live for Jesus — he made us for himself — when we really begin to fall in love with him, to eat, drink and sleep Jesus, when we can say, "I live, no, not I, but Christ lives in me," like Paul and Mary, we will have learned the secret of life. We will have learned Glory Spout living. We will be seats of wisdom.

We will have trials. We'll have all kinds of trials. In fact, right now many, many people are going through tremendous trials, but the answer is praising God, hanging in there, clinging to the cross, more prayer, more praise, looking to the

Lord in a Paul and Silas fashion, in a Peter and John fashion, in a Stephen fashion, and we will have quick resurrections, quick answers, quick wisdom, new victories that we never dreamed of before. The trials will be intense. They will become more and more intense because the Lord would have us become stronger and stronger. He will walk with us as a stranger to see whether we will still hang in there, and if we do we'll have "resurrectionitis." We'll know the victory. That is what the Lord said: "I want you to have a bridal love for me. My mother will teach you how to cling to the cross; she will show you how to keep the great commandment; she will show you how to keep your eyes on me; she will show you how to love."

A lot of people have problems with prayer. They say, "I can't pray." The problem, I submit is not prayer: the problem is love. Prayer is but the expression of love. When you love someone, the loved one is always on your mind; you dream about the beloved. The problem with us, if we are to be honest about it, is that we don't love the Lord with our whole heart and soul. We don't really believe that the great commandment is the summary of the Law and the prophets. We don't really love like Mary loved Jesus or like Paul loved Jesus or like Stephen loved Jesus or like Basilea Schlink loves Jesus. This is the problem.

Nietzsche, the German philosopher whose writings influenced Adolf Hitler, once said: "If you Christians acted as if you were risen, as if you were victorious, I too would become a believer. But I don't see that in you. I see sadness . . . rather than the joy and the power of the risen Lord."

One hesitation you may have with regard to learning from Mary how to be a seat of wisdom is that this seems to honor Mary too much, perhaps making an idol of her. But that is missing the point. "My mother," Jesus would say, "is the Seat of Wisdom par excellence, but I want the same for you." Once people came to Jesus and said, "Your mother and your brothers are outside." And Jesus looked at his disciples and said, "Here are my mother and my brothers and my sisters. Whoever hears the word of God and keeps it, whoever does the will of my Father, he is my mother and my brother and my sister." What Jesus wants is as close a relationship with you and with me as he has with his mother. That is why he sends us to her. "Learn from her. Learn to be that close. I want to be as close to you as I was to her. I live in you as I lived in her. I want to make you a temple where my Father and I and the Holy Spirit can live. I want to make you Christ-bearers as she was. Learn from Mary and learn what you are called to be."

So to look at Mary, in one sense, is really not all that different from looking at Basilea Schlink or Kathryn Kuhlman — people who are filled with the Lord, tuned in to the Lord, never drifting, so that the power and the wisdom of the Lord constantly flow through them. They are seats of wisdom, and we need to look at them so that we, in turn, can become seats of wisdom.

Think about the wedding at Cana — a desperate situation — but God's glory was poured down nevertheless. Mary asked Jesus to work a miracle and even though he said it wasn't his time, because of her request and faith, he did it. The glory of the Lord came through. This was Glory Spout living, quick resurrection. This is the same power we have as Christians.

An opposite situation is contained in the phrase from the Gospel "We piped a tune to you and you wouldn't dance, we sang dirges to you and you wouldn't mourn." We don't want to hear it; we drift away. Our ears are closed. Our eyes are closed, and so God cannot give us what he wants to give us. He will not force us. He is a perfect gentleman. And because he is a gentleman, he won't bang down the door. He will just knock gently. He will never speak if someone else is talking. He just invites and we have to, in love, open up and want him to come in. Then we have bridal love. We have Glory Spout living; we have quick victories.

One of the titles of Mary in Christian tradition is "Spouse of the Holy Spirit." This is one of my favorite titles for her; it says it all. To be a spouse of the Holy Spirit — that is what you and I are called to be. Don't look at the title and say,

"Mary, Spouse of the Holy Spirit. That's idolatry!" That is to miss the point. Say rather, "Mary was the Spouse of the Holy Spirit. That is what I'm called to be. Jesus wants a bridal love with me, just as he had with Kathryn Kuhlman. Kathryn Kuhlman told people to go home. "The Lord wants to heal in your church, in your town." It's the same Lord who wants to save all his people and heal all his people. You can learn to be spouses of the Holy Spirit, too.

Tomorrow you may have all kinds of trials, probably more than usual because of reading this. But remember what I said. If you want to live under the Glory Spout and you say, "Yes, Lord, I'm going to live under the Glory Spout," he will as in Sirach 4 "walk with you as a stranger." He will say: "Have you learned the principle? Will you keep your eyes always on me? I want to tell you, you will always be able to see me. I promise I will always give you a view of me risen from the dead. I may walk as a stranger with you, but if you look attentively you will always be able to see and feel my presence. Can you do that? As I send trials to you, as I test you, as I walk with you as a stranger, will you stay under the Glory Spout? What will you do as I test you like I tested Paul and Silas and Peter and John and Stephen? Will you run away? Will you scream? Will you shout at the Sanhedrin? Will you say 'not fair'? Or will you trust my Spirit to act for you? Will you look at me risen from the dead in glory? Will you let me win a quick victory?" Here in Providence, Rhode Island, Jesus has taught us over and over again to go to his mother, to learn from her. We've learned in the prayer meetings, in ministry meetings with prophecies and words of Scripture and verifications, to go to Mary. We would be untrue to the Holy Spirit, we would be untrue to our prayer experience to deny this. We would be false to everything we have learned from the Holy Spirit if we were to say anything else. When we have obeyed Jesus in this regard, when we have learned the wisdom of effectively going to his mother, miracles have happened. When we've not, we have seen other things happen. The same thing has been true in individual prayer, community prayer, and in every ministry. It is simply being true to the Spirit to recognize clearly once and for all that Jesus has often sent us to the school of his mother to learn how to be seats of wisdom, to learn bridal love, to learn to be what we are called to be. I think this parallels the eighth chapter of the decree on the Church in Vatican Council II. It says something to that effect, and it has been our experience, a verification if you will, of the teaching of the Council fathers. Let me give you an example of what happens when we obey this word. Recently, August 15th happened to fall on a Friday, a prayer meeting night. We asked ourselves whether we should have a Mass and a teaching on Mary. On Friday nights, we have a lot of non-Catholics at our meeting. What were we to do? Well, we felt that the Lord was telling us to have a Mass, to be true to our calling. We are a parish, anyhow, and we needed to have a parish Mass. We boldly went forward. We had a Mass in honor of the Assumption, a mystery very difficult for most Protestants to understand, and we had a very beautiful teaching on Mary. Unknown to us, the whole chaplain formation school at the Naval Training Station at Newport decided to come to a charismatic prayer meeting that night and they were there in the audience. If we had known it, we might have acted differently, but we didn't, thank God. After the Mass was over that night, this group of chaplains, mostly Protestant, came up to us as a body and, visibly moved, said that this was one of the greatest religious experiences of their lives. Because we had been true to what we had heard the Lord calling us to do, we had tried to raise up Mary as an example of Glory Spout living. Many Catholics are afraid of being what they are. Cardinal Suenens, in his directives on Church Renewal, has often said, "Be what you are." In ecumenical dialogue, where Cardinal Suenens excels, he is saying it is short-sighted not to be what you are and as Catholics, you have a great tradition of coming to the Lord through Mary. Don't deny that. Affirm that. Protestants are looking to you to show them what this means, and when you are what you are, when you don't deny that, when you are true to your tradition and to your origins, the

Holy Spirit will do great things. Through his Spouse, he will continue to make Jesus live. That has been our experience. When we obey the Lord in this regard, we see tremendous things. Just recently, a Protestant couple in the community heard a teaching about appropriating the heart of Mary. They were open to the inspiration of the Spirit in this teaching. They had a tremendous religious experience and learned to love Jesus with a new heart. The same is true for us all. I just beg you to listen to this word. It's a word from the Spirit. For me not to say this would be to be untrue to everything I've heard. So I beg you to hear this word. It means life if you obey it. You will see miracles happen if you follow this. If you don't, well, you won't see that much life.

I'd like to address another question we often hear. Where have the charisms of the Spirit been over the centuries? It is as if a big vacuum existed somewhere between the early Church and the present charismatic renewal. I don't know the full answer to that, but I would like you to take a look at the last century, the nineteenth, which was supposedly a non-charismatic century. Let's take a look at Lourdes in the nineteenth century, one of the greatest charismatic places of all times. There were conversions and healings, prophecies, changes of life, huge crowds — one hundred thousand a week, greater than all the Notre Dame charismatic conferences put together. Why can't we link the nineteenth and the twentieth centuries together? We want now, in the false ecumenical thrust that many of us get caught up in, to deny these things, to cut our origins and to start off as if everything began yesterday. Why? This is charismatic snobbery. Mary at Lourdes was the only Catholic charismatic of the last century with prophecy, healings, and conversions; she was keeping the charismatic gifts alive. We must learn in simple wisdom to put together what the Lord has done, to build a second story on the foundation that has been there on the first story. God wants us to learn bridal love from this tradition of Christian mysticism, if you will. You can learn to be a seat of wisdom from a Basilea Schlink and I suggest you do. You can learn bridal love from a Kathryn Kuhlman and I suggest you do. But the best way to learn is through Catholic devotion to Mary. This is a purer way.

I'd like to give some practical suggestions as to how we might do this. First of all, ask Jesus to teach you. If you find some of the things I'm saying difficult, I beg you to go to Jesus in prayer and ask him about it. Don't take my word for it. Ask him to teach you. I'll rest the case there. The second thing I'd suggest is to be ready to hear what the Spirit is saying. Learn some of the signals he may be giving you. For example, if in prayer you turn to the book of Esther, or the book of Judith, or a book telling the story of Deborah or of the wise woman who dropped a stone on the enemy's head (Judges 9:50-56), perhaps he is speaking to you about the woman's role in Christian faith. If he keeps giving you passages from the Book of Wisdom that talk about wisdom as a "she," undoubtedly the Spirit is talking to you about Mary, particularly if this happens over and over again. Our deliverance ministry has learned to tap these kinds of secrets and when they get words like that, to beg Mary's intercession. Quick deliverance comes setting people free, and inner healings occur of very great power. So be open to those tips. The third thing is to ask Mary to teach you all about Jesus. Try to appropriate her heart. Ask Mary to give you her attitude toward Jesus. Try appropriating her attitude and see what happens to you. Finally, take Mary as an intercessor, not just as a model. Here is where we depart from seats of wisdom such as Basilea Schlink or Kathryn Kuhlman, for example. Besides being a perfect model, the Seat of Wisdom, par excellence, Mary is also an intercessor. We Catholics believe that we can intercede for one another. Everybody believes that. I can intercede for you; you can intercede for me. I believe that when I die and when you die, we're going to enter into the resurrection, and we can continue to intercede as Jesus is interceding before the throne of God. We can continue interceding for one another, and I hope that when I die, you will intercede for me. We believe this is true of the saints. We believe that it is true of Mary. Intercession is a fact. It is scriptural to turn to the saints that they may be intermediaries. Look at Cana. Jesus was not about to work his first miracle. He said it wasn't his time, even when Mary first asked him. However, she persisted, like the woman nagging the judge in Luke 18:1-11. She told the servants, "Do whatever he tells you," and Jesus was swayed. He worked his first miracle out of due time. That is intercession. Cana is a perfect example of the power of Mary's intercession. Go to her. Ask her to intercede for you. See what happens in your life. The Lord has given us a great gift; he has given us everything he ever had including, at the cross, his mother when he said, "Woman, there is your son . . . there is your mother" (*John 19:26-27*). He is still sending her to help us love him more. If we would truly be Christlike in every regard, we will have Christ's own heart toward his mother.

MARY:
Pathway to Fruitfulness   1.95

John Randall, STD., Helen P. Hawkinson, Sharyn Malloy. Mary is shown to be an exemplar of fruitful Christian living in her role as model relative, suffering servant and seat of wisdom. Her growing role as mediator between Catholics and Protestants is also highlighted.

FORMED BY HIS WORD:
Scriptural Patterns of Prayer   1.95

Rev. Malcolm Cornwell, C.P. Commentary on St. Luke; a set of teachings suitable for people seeking guidance in prayer.

JONAH:
Spirituality of a Runaway Prophet   1.75

Roman Ginn, o.c.s.o. While acquiring a new appreciation for this very human prophet, we come to see that his story is really our own. It reveals a God whose love is unwavering yet demanding, for if we are to experience the freedom of mature Christians, we must enter the darkness of the tomb with Christ, as Jonah did, in order to rise to new life.

POOR IN SPIRIT:
Awaiting All From God   1.75

Cardinal Garrone. Not a biography of the Mother Teresa of her age, this spiritual account of Jeanne Jugan's complete and joyful abandonment to God leads us to a vibrant understanding of spiritual and material poverty.

DESERT SILENCE:
A Way of Prayer for an Unquiet Age   1.75

Rev. Alan J. Placa. The pioneering efforts of the men and women of the early church who went out into the desert to find union with the Lord has relevance for those of us today who are seeking the pure uncluttered desert place within to have it filled with the loving silence of God's presence.

Order from your bookstore or
LIVING FLAME PRESS, Locust Valley, N.Y. 11560

PRAYING WITH SCRIPTURE IN THE HOLY LAND:
Daily Meditations With the Risen Jesus
2.25

Msgr. David E. Rosage. Herein is offered a daily meeting with the Risen Jesus in those Holy Places which He sanctified by His human presence. Three hundred and sixty-five scripture texts are selected and blended with the pilgrimage experiences of the author, a retreat master, and well-known writer on prayer.

DISCOVERING PATHWAYS TO PRAYER
1.75

Msgr. David E. Rosage. Following Jesus was never meant to be dull, or worse, just duty-filled. Those who would aspire to a life of prayer and those who have already begun, will find this book amazingly thorough in its scripture-punctuated approach.

"A simple but profound book which explains the many ways and forms of prayer by which the person hungering for closer union with God may find him." **Emmnauel Spillane, O.C.S.O., Abbot, Our Lady of the Holy Trinity Abbey, Huntsville, Utah.**

REASONS FOR REJOICING
Experiences in Christian Hope
1.75

Rev. Kenneth J. Zanca. The author asks: "Do we really or rarely have a sense of excitement, mystery, and wonder in the presence of God?" His book offers a path to rejuvenation in Christian faith, hope, and love. It deals with prayer, forgiveness, worship and other religious experiences in a learned and penetrating, yet simple, non-technical manner. **Religion Teachers' Journal.**

"It is a refreshing Christian approach to the Good News, always emphasizing the love and mercy of God in our lives, and our response to that love in Christian hope." **Brother Patrick Hart, Secretary to the late Thomas Merton.**

CONTEMPLATIVE PRAYER:
Problems and An Approach for the Ordinary Christian
1.75

Rev. Alan J. Placa. This inspiring book covers much ground: the struggle of prayer, growth in familiarity with the Lord and the sharing process. In addition, he clearly outlines a method of contemplative prayer for small groups based on the belief that private communion with God is essential to, and must precede, shared prayer. The last chapter provides model prayers, taken from our Western heritage, for the enrichment of private prayer experience.

THE ONE WHO LISTENS:
A Book of Prayer   2.25

Rev. Michael Hollings and Etta Gullick. Here the Spirit speaks
through men and women of the past (St. John of the Cross, Thomas
More, Dietrich Bonhoeffer), and present (Michel Quoist, Mother
Teresa, Malcolm Boyd). There are also prayers from men of other
faiths such as Muhammed and Tagore. God meets us where we are
and since men share in sorrow, joy and anxiety, *their* prayers are *our*
prayers. This is a book that will be outworn, perhaps, but never
outgrown.

ENFOLDED BY CHRIST:
An Encouragement to Pray   1.95

Rev. Michael Hollings. This book helps us toward giving our lives to
God in prayer yet at the same time remaining totally available to
our fellowman — a difficult but possible feat. Father's sharing of his
own difficulties and his personal approach convince us that "if he
can do it, we can." We find in the author a true spiritual guardian
and friend.

PETALS OF PRAYER:
Creative Ways to Pray   1.50

Rev. Paul Sauve. "*Petals of Prayer is an extremely practical book for
anyone who desires to pray but has difficulty finding a method for
so doing. At least 15 different methods of prayer are described and
illustrated in simple, straightforward ways, showing they can be
contemporary even though many of them enjoy a tradition of hundreds of years. In an excellent introductory chapter, Fr. Sauve states
that the best 'method' of prayer is the one which unites us to
God. . . . Father Sauve masterfully shows how traditional methods
of prayer can be very much in tune with a renewed church.*" St.
Anthony Messenger.

Order from your bookstore or
LIVING FLAME PRESS, Locust Valley, N.Y. 11560

CRISIS OF FAITH:
Invitation to Christian Maturity   1.50

Rev. Thomas Keating, o.c.s.o. How to hear ourselves called to discipleship in the Gospels is Abbot Thomas' important and engrossing message. As Our Lord forms His disciples, and deals with His friends or with those who come asking for help in the Gospels, we can receive insights into the way He is forming or dealing with us in our day to day lives.

IN GOD'S PROVIDENCE:
The Birth of a Catholic Charismatic Parish   1.50

Rev. John Randall. The engrossing story of the now well-known Word of God Prayer Community in St. Patrick's Parish, Providence, Rhode Island, as it developed from Father Randall's first adverse reaction to the budding Charismatic Movement to today as it copes with the problems of being a truly pioneer Catholic Charismatic Parish.

"This splendid little volume bubbles over with joy and peace, with 'Spirit' and work." **The Priest.**

SOURCE OF LIFE:
The Eucharist and Christian Living   1.50

Rev. Rene Voillaume. A powerful testimony to the vital part the Eucharist plays in the life of a Christian. It is a product of a man for whom Christ in the Eucharist is nothing less than all.

SEEKING PURITY OF HEART:
The Gift of Ourselves to God   illus. 1.25

Joseph Breault. For those of us who feel that we do not live up to God's calling, that we have sin of whatever shade within our hearts. This book shows how we can begin a journey which will lead from our personal darkness to wholeness in Christ's light — a purity of heart. Clear, practical help is given us in the constant struggle to free ourselves from the deceptions that sin has planted along all avenues of our lives.

Order from your bookstore or
LIVING FLAME PRESS, Locust Valley, N.Y. 11560

PROMPTED BY THE SPIRIT   2.25

Rev. Paul Sauvé. A handbook by a Catholic Charismatic Renewal national leader for all seriously concerned about the future of the renewal and interested in finding answers to some of the problems that have surfaced in small or large prayer groups. It is a call to all Christians to find answers with the help of a wise Church tradition as transmitted by her ordained ministers. The author has also written *Petals of Prayer/Creative Ways to Pray.*

THE BOOK OF REVELATION:
What Does It Really Say?   1.75

Rev. John Randall, S.T.D. The most discussed book of the Bible today is examined by a scripture expert in relation to much that has been published on the Truth. A simply written and revealing presentation.

. . . AND I WILL FILL THIS HOUSE WITH GLORY:
Renewal Within a Suburban Parish   1.50

Rev. James A. Brassil. This book helps answer the questions: What is the Charismatic Renewal doing for the Church as a whole? and What is the prayer group doing for the parish? With a vibrant prayer life and a profound devotion to the Eucharist, this Long Island prayer group has successfully endured the growing pains inherent to the spiritual life, the fruit of which is offered to the reader.

Books by Venard Polusney, O. Carm.

UNION WITH THE LORD IN PRAYER
Beyond Meditation To Affective Prayer Aspiration And Contemplation .85

"A magnificent piece of work. It touches on all the essential points of Contemplative Prayer. Yet it brings such a sublime subject down to the level of comprehension of the 'man in the street,' and in such an encouraging way."
Abbott James Fox, O.C.S.O. (former superior of Thomas Merton at the Abbey of Gethsemani)

ATTAINING SPIRITUAL MATURITY FOR CONTEMPLATION (According to St. John of the Cross) .85

"I heartily recommend this work with great joy that at last the sublime teachings of St. John of the Cross have been brought down to the understanding of the ordinary Christian without at the same time watering them down. For all (particularly for charismatic Christians) hungry for greater contemplation."
Rev. George A. Maloney, S.J., Editor of Diakonia, Professor of Patristics and Spirituality, Fordham University.

THE PRAYER OF LOVE ... THE ART OF ASPIRATION
1.50

"It is the best book I have read which evokes the simple and loving response to remain in love with the Lover. To read it meditatively, to imbibe its message of love, is to have it touch your life and become part of what you are."
Mother Dorothy Guilbuilt, O. Carm., Superior General, Lacombe, La.

Order from your bookstore or
LIVING FLAME PRESS, Locust Valley, N.Y. 11560

LIVING FLAME PRESS
BOX 74, LOCUST VALLEY, N.Y. 11560

Quantity

_____	Mary: Pathway to Fruitfulness — 1.95
_____	The Judas Within — 1.95
_____	Formed by His Word — 1.95
_____	Jonah — 1.75
_____	Poor in Spirit — 1.75
_____	Desert Silence — 1.75
_____	Praying With Scripture in the Holy Land — 2.25
_____	Discovering Pathways to Prayer — 1.75
_____	Reasons for Rejoicing — 1.75
_____	Contemplative Prayer — 1.75
_____	The One Who Listens — 2.25
_____	Enfolded by Christ — 1.95
_____	Petals of Prayer — 1.50
_____	Crisis of Faith — 1.50
_____	In God's Providence — 1.50
_____	Source of Life — 1.50
_____	Seeking Purity of Heart — 1.25
_____	Prompted by the Spirit — 2.25
_____	The Book of Revelation — 1.75
_____	And I Will Fill This House With Glory — 1.50
_____	Union With the Lord in Prayer — .85
_____	Attaining Spiritual Maturity — .85
_____	The Prayer of Love — 1.50

QUANTITY ORDER: DISCOUNT RATES

For convents, prayer groups, etc.: $10 to $25 = 10%;
$26 to $50 = 15%; over $50 = 20%. Booksellers: 40%, 30 days net.

NAME _____

ADDRESS _____

CITY_____ STATE_____ ZIP_____

☐ *Payment enclosed. Kindly include $.50 postage and handling on order up to $5.00. Above that, include 10% of total up to $20.*
  •Then 7% of total. Thank you.